Windows® 8 For Seniors

FOR

DUMMIES®

by Mark Justice Hinton

WILEY

John Wiley & Sons, Inc.

Windows® 8 For Seniors For Dummies®

Published by
John Wiley & Sons, Inc.
111 River Street
Hoboken, NJ 07030-5774
www.wiley.com

Copyright © 2012 by John Wiley & Sons, Inc., Hoboken, New Jersey

Published by John Wiley & Sons, Inc., Hoboken, New Jersey

Published simultaneously in Canada

For general information on our other products and services, please contact our Customer Care Department within the U.S. at 877-762-2974, outside the U.S. at 317-572-3993, or fax 317-572-4002.

For technical support, please visit www.wiley.com/techsupport.

Wiley publishes in a variety of print and electronic formats and by print-on-demand. Some material included with standard print versions of this book may not be included in e-books or in print-on-demand. If this book refers to media such as a CD or DVD that is not included in the version you purchased, you may download this material at http://booksupport.wiley.com. For more information about Wiley products, visit www.wiley.com.

Library of Congress Control Number: 2012948924

ISBN 978-1-118-12028-6 (pbk); ISBN 978-1-118-23803-5 (ebk); ISBN 978-1-118-26273-3 (ebk); ISBN 978-1-118-22460-1 (ebk)

Manufactured in the United States of America

10 9 8 7 6 5 4 3 2

WILEY

About the Author

A computerist for more than 30 years, **Mark Justice Hinton** has written books on digital photography as well as on three versions of Microsoft Windows: Vista, Windows 7, and Windows 8. This is his third title in the *For Seniors* series. He has taught thousands of students since 1988 in classes for the University of New Mexico Division of Continuing Education. Mark writes a blog on computer topics at www.mjhinton.com/help. He posts favorite photos, as well, at www.photosbymjh.com.

Dedication

To New Mexico/The Land of Enchantment

Author's Acknowledgments

It took a lot of people to put this book into your hands. The author gets the fame, the fans, and the fat check, but he couldn't do it without many other people, too many of whom go unnamed here. Thanks to everyone at Wiley for their part in producing this book. Foremost, I'm grateful to Susan Pink, editor. Susan combines experience and skill with an unflappable good nature. It was my good fortune and pleasure to work with her. Special thanks to editorial manager Jodi Jensen, my acquisitions editor, Amy Fandrei, technical editor Russ Mullen, and editorial assistant Leslie Saxman. My deepest thanks, always, to Merri Rudd, photographer and writer, as well as mi corazón for more than thirty years.

peace,
mjh

Publisher's Acknowledgments

We're proud of this book; please send us your comments at http://dummies.custhelp.com. For other comments, please contact our Customer Care Department within the U.S. at 877-762-2974, outside the U.S. at 317-572-3993, or fax 317-572-4002.

Some of the people who helped bring this book to market include the following:

Acquisitions and Editorial

Project Editor: Susan Pink

Acquisitions Editor: Amy Fandrei

Copy Editor: Susan Pink

Technical Editor: Russ Mullen

Editorial Manager: Jodi Jensen

Editorial Assistant: Amanda Foxworth

Sr. Editorial Assistant: Cherie Case

Cover Photo: © Datacraft Co. Ltd/Getty Images

Cartoons: Rich Tennant (www.the5thwave.com)

Composition Services

Sr. Project Coordinator: Kristie Rees

Layout and Graphics: Carl Byers, Carrie A. Cesavice, Corrie Niehaus

Proofreader: Christine Sabooni

Indexer: Dakota Indexing

Publishing and Editorial for Technology Dummies

Richard Swadley, Vice President and Executive Group Publisher

Andy Cummings, Vice President and Publisher

Mary Bednarek, Executive Acquisitions Director

Mary C. Corder, Editorial Director

Publishing for Consumer Dummies

Kathleen Nebenhaus, Vice President and Executive Publisher

Composition Services

Debbie Stailey, Director of Composition Services

Table of Contents

Introduction

*W*indows 8 is the latest generation of Microsoft's operating system, the master program that makes a computer useful and provides support to other programs, including word processors, photo viewers, and web browsers. Much as an education equips you to read a novel or play a game, Windows 8 equips your computer to perform a wide range of activities. You can use Windows 8 and other software (or *apps*) to read or write a novel, play games or music, and stay in touch with friends and family around the world.

As Windows has evolved over the past 30 years, so have computers — the *hardware*. Today, you can buy a computer as small as a paperback book, and even such a little computer is unimaginably more powerful than (and a fraction of the cost of) computers just 10 years ago. The hardware consists of the screen, as well as optional components such as a keyboard and a mouse.

You don't need much time with a computer to conclude that there has to be an easier way to do things. At times, computers seem overly complex and inscrutable. Have you used a cellphone lately? Or a TV remote control? Why are the controls on every microwave oven different? Why does every new tool offer countless options you don't want that obscure the ones you do want? Well, I don't have the answers to those questions, but I do have step-by-step instructions for many tasks you want to perform using Windows 8.

After 34 years working with computers, I find that they reward patience, curiosity, and a little methodical exploration. Seniors, in particular, know that learning never really stops and that learning new things keep one young, at least figuratively. By the end of this book, you may be a multitasking computerist performing virtual gymnastics with Windows 8. On the other hand, if this book helps you do only one thing— using e-mail, browsing the Web, or enjoying photos or music— that one useful thing may be all you need.

About This Book

Age is just a number. This book is intended for anyone getting started with Windows 8 who wants step-by-step instructions without a lot of discussion. The *Get ready to . . .* bullets at the beginning of each chapter lead you to practical tasks. Numerous figures with notes show you the computer screen as you progress through the steps. Reading this book is like having an experienced friend stand behind you as you use Windows 8 . . . someone who never takes control of the computer away from you.

Conventions Used in This Book

This book uses certain conventions to highlight important information and help you find your way around:

➠ **Different methods for performing steps**: In general, you can complete a step in three ways. I list the choices as follows:

- **Mouse:** If you have a mouse, follow these instructions.

- **Touchscreen:** You may be able to touch your screen to perform tasks.

- **Keyboard:** Keyboard shortcuts are often the fastest way to do something.

When you have a choice between these methods, experiment to determine which is easiest for you.

➡ **Tip icons:** Point out helpful suggestions related to tasks in the steps lists.

➡ **Bold:** I use bold for figure references and also when you have to type something onscreen using the keyboard

Many figures have notes or other markings to draw your attention to a specific part of the figure. The text tells you what to look for; the figure notes help you find it.

➡ **Website addresses:** If you bought an e-book, website address are live links. In the text, website addresses look like this: www.win8mjh.com. See Chapter 6 for information on browsing the Web.

➡ **Options and buttons:** Although Windows 8 often uses lowercase in options and on buttons, I capitalize the text for emphasis. That way, you can find a button labeled Save Now, even though onscreen it appears as *Save now*.

What You're Not to Read

You can work through this book from beginning to end or simply look at the table of contents and find the content you need to solve a problem or help you learn a new skill whenever you need it. The steps in each task get you where you want to go quickly without a lot of technical explanation. In no time, you'll start picking up the skills you need to become a confident Windows 8 user.

Technology always comes with its own terms and concepts, but you don't need to learn another language to use a computer. You don't need any prior experience with computers or Windows. Step-by-step instructions guide you through specific tasks, such as accessing the news or playing a game. These steps provide just the information you need for the task at hand.

Foolish Assumptions

I assume that you have a computer and want clear, brief, step-by-step instructions on getting things done with Windows 8. I assume also that you want to know just what you need to know, just when you need to know it. This isn't Computers 101. This is Practical Windows 8. As an old friend of mine said, "I don't want to make a watch; I just want to know what time it is."

How This Book Is Organized

This book is divided into four parts to help you find what you need. You can read from cover to cover or just jump to the page that interests you.

➠ **Part I: Getting to Know Windows 8.** In Chapter 1, you turn on the computer and get comfortable with essential parts of Windows 8, such as the Start screen, as well as how to use a mouse, touchscreen, or keyboard. Explore features of Windows 8 apps in Chapter 2. To customize Windows 8 to work better for you, turn to Chapter 3. In Chapter 4, you create and modify user accounts settings, such as passwords. Discover the desktop, a workspace for running apps created before Windows 8, in Chapter 5.

➠ **Part II: Windows 8 and the Web.** Use the Web to stay current and keep in touch. Turn to Chapter 6 to use Microsoft Internet Explorer to browse the Web. Send and receive e-mail in Chapter 7. Want to stay in touch with family and friends using such popular services as Facebook? See Chapter8.

➠ **Part III: Having Fun with Windows 8.** If you haven't been having any fun until now, I've failed you. Expand your tools and toys in Chapter 9 by connecting to Microsoft Store to install new apps. In Chapter 10, you enjoy photos on Windows 8 and put your own photos on the computer. If you want to listen to music and watch a movie, see Chapter 11.

➠ **Part IV: Beyond the Basics.** In Chapter 12, you learn about the care and feeding of Windows 8, which requires a little maintenance now and then. Find out how to connect a printer and other hardware, such as a mouse and a second screen, in Chapter 13. Do you think "a place for everything and everything in its place"? Chapter 14 is where you organize your documents. You back up your files to insure against loss and refresh Windows 8 when it gets cranky, all in Chapter 15.

Where to Go from Here

Scan the table of contents or the index for a topic that interests you most. Or just turn the page and start at the beginning. It's your book.

Comments and suggestions are welcome. Write me at mark@ mjhinton.com. For supplemental material and updates, visit the book's website at www.win8mjh.com. as well as www.dummies. com/go/windows8.

Part I

Getting to Know Windows 8

The 5th Wave   By Rich Tennant

"Well, she's fast on the keyboard and knows how to load the printer, but she just sort of plays with the mouse."

Getting in Touch with Windows 8

With Windows 8, Microsoft created a grand version of Windows, its flagship *operating system* (the master program for any computer). You can use Windows 8 on a wide range of devices, from a smartphone to a big-screen TV entertainment system: one size fits most. You can not only use the same programs with a range of hardware but also access the documents you create (such as photos and e-mail — files and data, to nerds) from any Windows-based computer, giving you extraordinary freedom of choice and mobility.

Although countless companies create programs you may use, Microsoft attempts to make similar functions consistent across different programs. For example, opening a document or e-mailing a photo to a friend involves the same steps regardless of the programs you use. You don't have to learn a different way of doing common tasks in each program. This consistency will serve you well when using Windows 8 and other new programs.

In this chapter, you start your computer and work with the *Start screen*, the dashboard for Windows 8. You explore options for using the Start screen with your *hardware* (the computer and related devices). Then you exit Windows 8 and go right back in for more.

For those readers familiar with a previous version of Windows, note that the Start button and menu have been replaced by the new Start screen, and the desktop and taskbar are in a new location. See Chapter 5 for more information about the desktop.

 The easiest way to get Windows 8 is preinstalled on a new computer. If your current computer runs Windows 7, you can upgrade to Windows 8, although an older machine may lack newer functions, such as a touchscreen. Instructions for upgrading from a previous version of Windows are on the book's website at www.win8mjh.com. (See Chapter 6 for help on visiting that website and others.)

Tell Your Computer What to Do

How do you get Windows 8 to do what you want it to do? You can command a computer in many ways, depending on your equipment (hardware). For example, a desktop computer has different options from a handheld phone. You may have any or all of these choices:

➡ **Mouse**

➡ **Touchscreen**

➡ **Keyboard**

Another device for controlling Windows is a touchpad, which is commonly found on a laptop keyboard. You move your finger on the touchpad to move the pointer on the screen. You may also be able to control Windows using speech and a microphone. Microsoft Kinect is a device that enables you to control your computer with a wave of your hand. Welcome to the future!

If you have a computer with more than one of these devices, you might use one device exclusively or, more likely, vary your choice according to the task. Use whichever technique is easiest for you, but don't be afraid to experiment. In the next few sections, you discover the ins and outs of using all these methods of controlling Windows 8. Then you're ready to turn on your computer and use these methods.

 In the steps throughout this book, *choose* or *select* refers to using a mouse, the touchscreen, or a physical keyboard. *Drag* refers to using a mouse or a finger.

Move the Mouse

For many years, computers have had a mouse, which is a soap-bar-sized device that you move across a desk with your hand. Move the mouse and note how the arrow called a *mouse pointer* moves across the computer screen. A mouse has two or more buttons; some also have a scroll wheel between the buttons.

The following terms describe methods for using a mouse with Windows 8. In each, move the mouse first to position the pointer over a specified item before proceeding:

➡ **Click:** Move the on-screen arrow-shaped mouse pointer over a specified item and press and release the left mouse button: that's a click (sometimes called a left-click to distinguish it from a right-click).

➡ **Right-click:** Press and release the right mouse button to display available functions. Note that the word *click* by itself means use the left mouse button.

➡ **Drag:** Press and hold down the left mouse button, and then move the mouse pointer across the screen. When you want to move an object, you drag it. Release the mouse button to release the object.

 Watch for the word *click* to indicate using a mouse button and *roll* to indicate using the mouse wheel.

Touch the Screen

A *touchscreen*, as the name says, enables you to touch the screen to tell your computer what to do. You typically use one finger or two, although touchscreens may allow you to use all ten digits. In some cases, you can also use a special pen called a *stylus* instead of your finger. Tablet computers and some smartphones have touchscreens. Touchscreens are less common on desktop or laptop computers, but that situation is changing. Not sure what type of screen you have? When you have Windows 8 running, give the screen a poke with your index finger to see what happens.

The following terms refer to ways you interact with a touchscreen:

➡ **Tap:** Briefly touch the screen. You *select* an object, such as a button, by tapping it.

➡ **Drag:** Touch and hold your finger on the screen, then move your finger across the screen. You *move* an object, such as an onscreen playing card, by dragging it.

➡ **Swipe:** Touch and move your finger more quickly than with drag. You can swipe your finger across the screen from any of the four sides of the screen to display options and commands. You swipe pages to move forward or back. You may see the word *flick* instead of *swipe*. Some people insist that a flick is faster or shorter than a swipe, but let's not get caught up in that.

➡ **Pinch and unpinch:** Touch a finger and thumb or two fingers on the screen. Move your fingers closer to each other to *pinch* and away from each other to *unpinch*. Generally, a pinch reduces the size of something on the screen or shows more content on the screen. An unpinch (an ugly word) *zooms in*, increasing the size of something on-screen to show more detail.

Watch for the words *tap*, *swipe*, or *pinch* to indicate using your finger. Touch actions are often called *gestures*.

 See the section "View the Virtual Keyboard" if your computer doesn't have a physical keyboard, as is often the case with a touchscreen.

Use a Keyboard

A typewriter-like keyboard is a traditional device for controlling a computer and is especially useful when you must enter a lot of text. Special key combinations, called *shortcut keys*, are often the quickest way to do anything (though they require some memorization).

The following keys are particularly noteworthy. No offense intended to fans of keys not noted here. Although you won't use all these keys immediately, locate each one on your keyboard.

 Press indicates use the keyboard (physical or virtual) for the specified key or sequence of keys (just as *click* indicates a mouse action and *tap* indicates touch). Combinations of keys are not pressed simultaneously. Instead, press and hold the first key in the specified sequence, press the second key, then release both. (I explain exceptions to this method as necessary.)

➡ ⊞: Called the Windows key, this key is usually located on either side of the spacebar, which is the largest key. ⊞ works by itself, as you'll soon see, and also in combination with many other keys. Throughout the book, I specify these combinations where you might use them. There will be a quiz later. (Kidding! No quizzes.)

➡ **Tab:** Press the Tab key to highlight an item. Press Tab repeatedly to skip items you don't intend to select.

The keyboard can be used to select objects but is less direct than using touch or a mouse.

➡ **Arrow keys:** Press the arrow keys to move the cursor or selection of an object in the direction the keys point (left, right, up, or down). In some contexts, Tab and the right arrow do the same thing. Sorry to be vague, but context matters, at times.

➡ **Enter:** In most cases, the Enter key on the keyboard chooses a selection, much as clicking or tapping do. However, you may need to use the Tab key or an arrow key to select an item before pressing the Enter key.

➡ **Ctrl, Alt,** and **Shift keys:** These keys are used with other keys for commands. For example, press Ctrl+C to copy selected text or an object. (That is, while pressing and holding down the Ctrl key, press the C key — no need to press Shift for an uppercase C. Then release both keys.) The Shift key is used with another key for uppercase.

➡ **Backspace:** As you enter text, each press of Backspace erases the character to the left of the cursor.

➡ **Delete:** As you enter text, each press of the Delete key erases the character to the right of the cursor. On some keyboards, this key is labeled Del.

➡ **Function keys:** All keys function, but Function keys are labeled F1 through F12. You don't use these much in this book, but locate them. Laptops often have a separate Function Lock key to turn these keys on or off.

➡ **Page keys:** Locate the Home, End, Page Up, and Page Down keys for future reference. Use these to move the screen, a page, or the cursor.

View the Virtual Keyboard

Windows 8 can display a virtual keyboard on-screen. This feature is vital for devices that have a touchscreen and no physical keyboard. With a touchscreen, the virtual keyboard appears automatically when the *cursor* (a blinking vertical bar) indicates that you can enter text in a box. If the virtual keyboard doesn't appear automatically, you may also see a separate box floating above or below the text box. Tap that floating box to display the keyboard. To type using the keyboard, simply tap or click a letter, number, or symbol key.

Different types of virtual keyboards:

➠ The *standard layout* (also called QWERTY) appears automatically (see **Figure 1-1**). The Enter key changes depending on the context.

Standard layout

Figure 1-1

➠ The *uppercase layout,* shown in **Figure 1-2**, appears when you tap the Shift key on the standard layout.

Uppercase layout

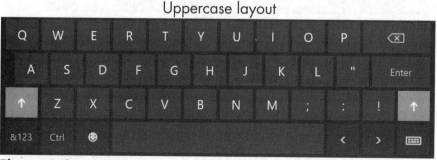

Figure 1-2

➠ The *numbers and symbols layout,* shown in **Figure 1-3,** appears when you tap the &123 key on the standard layout. Tap the &123 key again to return to the standard layout.

Numbers and symbols layout

Figure 1-3

➠ The control keys overlay (see **Figure 1-4**) appears on five keys on the standard layout when you tap the Ctrl key. The Ctrl keys are used in common tasks, such as copying (Ctrl+C) or moving (Ctrl+X) selected text. The overlay disappears automatically after you tap one of the control keys (A, Z, X, C, or V).

Ctrl keys layout

Figure 1-4

➠ The *smiley layout,* shown in **Figure 1-5,** appears when you tap the smiley face key. Tap the smiley face key again to return to the standard layout. (Smileys are also called *emoticons* or *emoji.*)

Smiley Keys layout

Figure 1-5

But wait! There's more. Tap the keyboard key, which is in the lower-right corner of any layout, to display the four options shown in **Figure 1-6**.

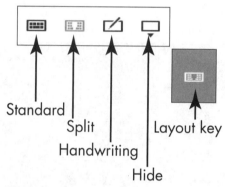

Standard
Split
Handwriting
Hide
Layout key

Figure 1-6

➠ Tap the standard button (shown in **Figure 1-6**) to return to the standard layout from the split or handwriting layout. (More on those two layouts next.)

➠ Tap the split button to view the *split keyboard layout,* shown in **Figure 1-7**. This layout is handy for typing with your thumbs while holding two sides of a tablet.

Split layout

Figure 1-7

➠ Tap the handwriting button to view the *handwriting layout,* shown in **Figure 1-8.** This layout enables you to write with a finger or a stylus (a special pen). Printing usually works better than script.

Handwriting layout

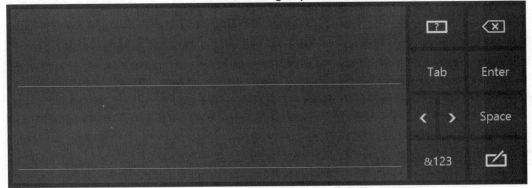

Figure 1-8

 If your touchscreen doesn't come with a stylus, you can buy one and use it instead of your finger for improved precision.

➠ Tap the last button to dismiss or hide the virtual keyboard.

Turn On Your Computer

1. Push the power button briefly and release it. Every computer has a power button. (When we can no longer turn them off, the machines win.) If you have a desktop computer tower, the power button is probably on the front of the tower. Otherwise, you might have to feel around the front and sides of the screen or near the hinges of a laptop. Typically, your computer will beep, some buttons will light, and the screen may flash a logo or a message that disappears before you can read it. (Just let that go.) Soon, you will see the first Windows 8 screen.

2. Turn on any separate hardware (such as a monitor or a printer).

The remaining steps in this section occur only when your computer is set up for the first time.

3. The first time you turn on your computer, a series of Windows Setup screens appear. On the initial screen, you select Language to Install, the Time and Currency Format, and the Keyboard or Input Method. Accept the defaults or change them appropriately, and then select the button labeled Next.

4. Select Install Now. (Note the option to Repair Your Computer, used if something goes wrong in the future.) The screen displays *Setup is starting*.

5. If you see a message asking you for a *product key* (a mix of 25 letters and numbers found on the back or bottom of your computer or on related paperwork), type those characters (hyphens are inserted automatically) and then select Next.

If your computer doesn't have a keyboard, as is the case with many tablet computers, see the preceding section "View the Virtual Keyboard" for information on how to type on-screen.

6. On the License Terms screen, select the check box next to I Accept the License Terms. Feel free to be the first person ever to read the terms before agreeing to them. (If you refuse to accept the terms, you can't use Windows 8.) Then select the Next. You may see an indication of the Windows 8 installation progress. Your computer may restart during this process, as well.

7. On the Personalize screen, select a background color for the most common screens, as shown in **Figure 1-9**. When you make a selection, the screen background changes to reflect your choice. Preview as many choices as you like.

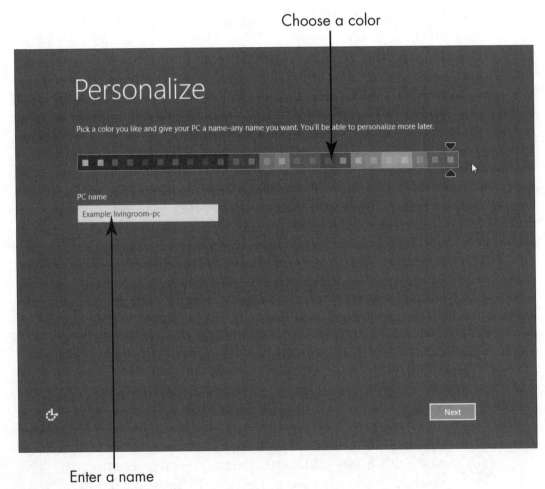

Choose a color

Enter a name

Figure 1-9

8. In the box under PC Name, type a short, simple name for your computer but don't use spaces. The name can be based on location (such as *office*) or computer brand (such as *Dell*) or something more creative (*Firefly* perhaps). This name is visible on a network, if you have one. Select Next.

 You can return to a previous screen (perhaps to confirm or change a selection) by selecting the Back button (an arrow in a circle, near the top-left corner of the screen). The Next button will move you forward again.

10. If a wireless Internet connection is available, you are prompted to select a connection and then select Connect. For now, select Connect to a Wireless Network Later. See Chapter 4 for information on connecting to a network.

11. On the Settings screen, select the Use Express Settings button for the easiest setup, as shown in **Figure 1-10**. If you choose the Customize button instead, you'll have to work through several screens of options.

 If this is the first time that Windows 8 has started on your computer, you must create a user account, even if no one else will use the machine. See Chapter 4 for details on creating and changing user accounts.

12. If you have an Internet connection, you see the Sign In to Your PC screen. (If you don't have an Internet connection, skip this step.) If you see the Sign in Without a Microsoft Account option, select it. You see a screen summarizing the differences between a Microsoft account and a local account. Select the Local Account button. (You use a Microsoft account in Chapter 4.)

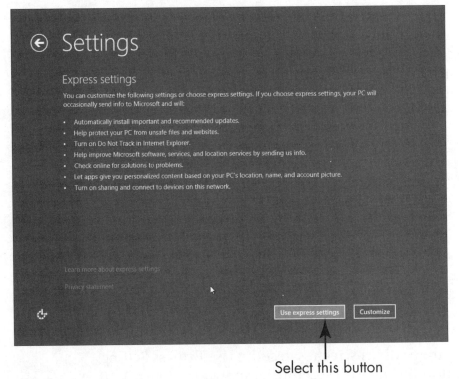

Select this button

Figure 1-10

13. In the User Name box, which is shown in **Figure 1-11**, type a short and simple name. Your user name appears throughout the system, from the log-in screen to the Start screen to the location containing all your documents. Use a simple, clear name. Your first name is just fine.

14. In the Password box, type a password. A password is an optional security measure. If you enter a password when you create your user account, that password is required each time you start the computer. If someone other than you tries to start your computer, he or she will have to know (or guess) the password to get into your files. (Don't put your password on a note stuck to the computer or nearby.)

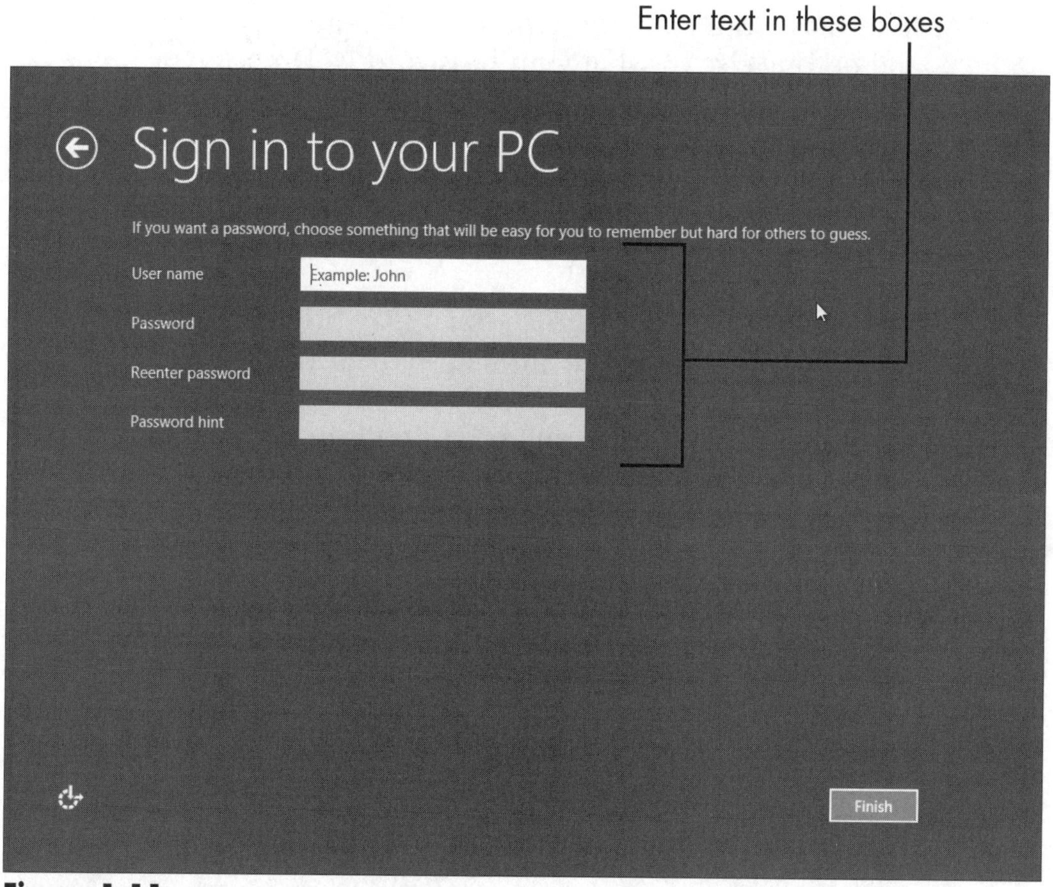

Enter text in these boxes

⊕ Sign in to your PC

If you want a password, choose something that will be easy for you to remember but hard for others to guess.

User name	Example: John
Password	
Reenter password	
Password hint	

Finish

Figure 1-11

For home computers, passwords may be unnecessary
unless you need to keep someone else in the house
out of your business. Laptop users should always create a password, however, because it is easy to lose a
laptop — don't make it easy for a thief to use your
computer.

15. In the Reenter Password box, type the same password
again.

16. In the Password Hint box, type a hint to remind yourself — and no one else — what your password is. Do not type the password itself here, or a hint such as *my first name.*

> I use my phone number as the hint. That way, if my computer is lost, someone might see my phone number and contact me. (I'm an optimist.)

17. Select the Finish button. The screen may briefly display *Finalizing your settings.* An animation demonstrates that you can move your mouse to any corner or, if you have a touchscreen, swipe from any edge. That's just the tip of the iceberg. The color of the screen and the text on-screen changes a few times to keep you mesmerized as setup finishes. Your PC will be ready in just a moment. Prepare to be awed. Behold, the Windows 8 Start screen, shown in **Figure 1-12.** (Your screen may be different than the one in this figure and those throughout the book.)

Figure 1-12

Check Out the Start Screen

1. Start your computer — if it isn't started already — and sign in to your user account. You'll see the Start screen, with your user name in the upper-right corner.

2. Examine the Start screen and note the colorful rectangular icons called *tiles*. These tiles represent available *apps* (short for application programs, an older term for programs or software). After you start to use the app tiles, they may display changing information, such as the current weather. (See Chapter 2 for information on using individual apps.)

3. Some tiles may extend beyond the right edge of the screen, (refer to **Figure 1-12**). To see the tiles that are off to the right, use one of the following methods to *scroll* (or move) the screen:

- **Mouse:** Move the mouse pointer to the right edge of the screen, far enough to see the screen move from right to left. You don't use any mouse buttons for this action. Move the mouse pointer to the left edge of the screen to scroll left. You can also roll the mouse wheel toward you to scroll right and away from you to scroll left.

- **Touchscreen:** Tap and hold down a finger in the area below the tiles. Drag from right to left. To scroll back, drag from left to right.

- **Keyboard:** Press the Page Down key to scroll right. Press the Page Up key to scroll left.

4. Use one of the following methods to display the charms bar (see **Figure 1-13**), which provides access to frequently used functions:

- **Mouse:** Move the mouse pointer to the upper-right or lower-right corner of the screen. Then move the mouse pointer out of the corner just a little to transform the charms bar from semitransparent to solid.

- **Touchscreen:** Swipe from the right edge of the screen to reveal the charms bar.

- **Keyboard:** Press ⊞+C. (Press and hold down the ⊞ key, press the C key, and then release both keys.)

Figure 1-13

 When the charms bar is visible, you'll see the time, day, and date in the lower left of the screen and an icon indicating whether your computer is connected to a network.

See Chapter 2 for information on setting the time.

5. Take a moment to observe the following charms:

- **Search:** Locate apps, documents, and more.

- **Share:** Send photos and more to family and friends.

- **Start:** Display the Start screen, which is useful if you aren't already there, which you are.

- **Devices:** Connect to printers and other devices such as flash drives and hard drives. See Chapter 13 for information on connecting and using a printer.

- **Settings:** Change the look and behavior of Windows 8 and individual apps.

 The charms bar gives you quick access to functions used in nearly every app.

6. You'll use all the charms eventually. For now, dismiss the charms bar using one of these methods:

- **Mouse:** Move the mouse pointer away from the charms bar or click the Start charm.

- **Touchscreen:** Tap the Start charm.

- **Keyboard:** Press ⊞+C.

Shut Down Your Computer

1. When you have finished using your computer for a while, you may want to shut down Windows 8. Begin by displaying the charms bar using one of these methods:

- **Mouse:** Move the mouse pointer to the upper-right or lower-right corner of the screen. (The charms bar appears semitransparent.) Then move the mouse pointer out of the corner just a little, until the charms bar becomes solid.

- **Touchscreen:** Swipe from the right edge of the screen to reveal the charms bar.

- **Keyboard:** Press ⊞+C.

2. Select the Settings charm, which is at the bottom of the charms bar (refer to **Figure 1-13**).

3. In the Settings panel, select the Power button. Available options will appear in a pop-up box, as shown in **Figure 1-14**. Some or all of the following options appear:

- **Shut Down:** This option exits Windows 8 and saves power by turning the computer off. In exiting Windows 8, Shut Down closes any apps that are currently running.

- **Sleep:** This option reduces the computer's power consumption without exiting Windows 8 or closing apps. As a result, when you wake the computer by moving the mouse or touching the screen or the keyboard, everything is exactly as you left it: apps and documents are open, if they were before Sleep.

- **Hibernate:** This option combines Sleep and Shut Down. Hibernate records which apps are running but also completely shuts down the computer. When you start the computer, Windows 8 opens all programs you were using, just like Sleep.

 Hibernate and Shut Down are equally green options — they save the same amount of power. Sleep is a little less green but saves time if you are returning to the middle of a task.

- **Restart:** Temporarily shuts down Windows 8 and turns it on again. Use Restart when Windows 8 asks you to or when Windows 8 is misbehaving.

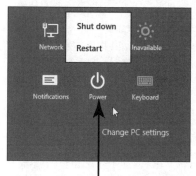

Select Power to see available options
Figure 1-14

4. Choose Shut Down to turn off the computer.

 On most computers, pressing the power switch also shuts down the computer. On a laptop, closing the lid may shut down the laptop or put it in sleep or hibernation mode.

 For a desktop computer, consider using a power strip to plug in the computer, the monitor, and the printer. After you shut down or hibernate the computer, turn off the power strip to save power.

Start Again on the Lock Screen

1. Turn on your computer. Every time you turn on your computer, the Lock screen appears, displaying the time, day, and date above a photo. (You change this photo in Chapter 3.) In **Figure 1-15,** note the *badge,* which is a small icon displaying bits of info about networking or an e-mail.

Badge   Lock screen

Figure 1-15

2. Dismiss the Lock screen with one of these methods:

- **Mouse:** Click anywhere, roll the wheel toward you, or drag the entire screen up.

- **Touchscreen:** Drag the entire screen up.

- **Keyboard:** Press any key.

3. If you don't use a password, wait briefly for the Start screen to appear. If you use a password, enter it with a physical or virtual keyboard. Then press Enter or select the arrow next to the password box to display the Start screen.

4. Take a break before reading Chapter 2.

Using the Start Screen and Apps

*T*he Windows 8 *Start screen* provides access to everything you do with Windows 8. It's the screen you will see most often and the first screen you see after signing in on the Lock screen. (See Chapter 1 for information on signing in.)

The Start screen is home to numerous programs, or *apps* (short for applications). An app performs a function or displays information. For example, the Weather app displays a local weather report (surprise!) and the Travel app lets you check on a flight and plan a trip. Apps can be simple or more complex, such as the Finance app for stock tracking.

Apps appear on the Start screen as *tiles*. A tile, which may be square or rectangular, displays the app's name and symbol or icon. A tile that displays changing information is called a *live tile*. An open app typically fills the entire screen, hiding everything else. However, some apps can be displayed side-by-side with a function called *snap*.

Get ready to . . .

Two categories of apps are available:

➠ *Windows 8 apps* open full screen. In general, Windows 8 apps are modern looking and rich with information. They are designed to work with touchscreens as well as with a mouse. Weather and Travel are the first two such apps you use in this chapter. (The News, Sports, and Finance apps function similarly to the Travel app, each with a unique focus.)

➠ *Desktop apps* always open with the desktop behind them. The *desktop* is a holdover from earlier versions of Windows. The desktop enables older programs to work with Windows 8, which is very different from previous versions of Windows. Most desktop apps don't have the look or consistent functions of Windows 8 apps. Desktop apps may not respond to touch as reliably as Windows 8 apps.

 Apps require a minimum *screen resolution*, which determines how much information the screen can display. Screen resolution is measured in *pixels*, or picture elements. Windows 8 requires a screen resolution no less than 1024 pixels wide by 768 pixels high. If your new Windows 8 computer has a higher screen resolution, you'll see more information — more tiles and more text — on the screen.

You select an app to use in one of two ways:

➠ **Mouse:** Move the mouse pointer over an app tile. Click the left mouse button to select the tile and open the app.

➠ **Touchscreen:** Tap the app tile with one of your fingers.

In this chapter, you open, close, and use some of the apps that come with Windows 8. You also switch between apps and the Start screen and switch directly between two apps. You find out how to search for apps not shown on the Start screen. Finally, you discover how to organize the Start screen by rearranging tiles.

See Chapter 9 for information on getting new apps from the Windows Store.

 Although some steps are specific to one app, most of the steps you follow in this chapter can be repeated in any app.

Open the Weather and Travel Apps

1. On the Start screen, which is shown in **Figure 2-1**, use a mouse or finger to select the tile labeled Weather. The Weather app's *splash screen* appears briefly with the app name.

Weather tile

Figure 2-1

2. The Weather app can determine your location from your network and automatically update your location if you travel with your computer from one city to another. If you see a screen asking *Do you want to turn on location services and allow Weather to use your location?* select Allow to enable the app to determine your location, or Block if you want to manually enter the location later.

3. Switch back to the Start screen using one of these methods:

- **Mouse:** Move the mouse pointer to the lower-left corner of the screen. A *thumbnail* (small image) of the Start screen appears, as shown in **Figure 2-2**. Click the left mouse button.

- **Touchscreen:** Swipe a finger from the right edge of the screen to display the charms bar. (For more on the charms bar, see Chapter 1.) Tap the Start button in the middle of the charms bar.

- **Keyboard:** Press the ⊞ key to suspend the Weather app temporarily and switch back to the Start screen.

Start screen thumbnail

Figure 2-2

Focus on the method you think is easiest. However, keep in mind that alternative methods of controlling your computer are always available.

4. On the Start screen, check to see if the Weather tile is displaying current weather information, as in **Figure 2-3**. The Weather app has a live tile, which displays changing information for a location (even the wrong location is okay for now). See "Add a Location in Weather" for information on setting your location.

Weather has a live tile

Figure 2-3

5. Switch back to the Weather app by selecting the Weather tile or by using one of the methods in Step 3, which alternate between the Start screen and the most recently open app. The Weather app reappears and takes up the full screen.

6. Switch back to the Start screen.

7. Select the Travel tile (look for a suitcase icon). To see this tile, you may have to move (*scroll*) the screen to the right using one of these methods:

- **Mouse:** With the mouse pointer anywhere, roll the mouse wheel toward you, or move the mouse pointer to the right edge of the screen without rolling the wheel. Keep moving the mouse to the right to continue scrolling. No mouse buttons are used for this operation. (To scroll left, roll the mouse wheel away from you or move the mouse pointer to the left edge of the screen.)

- **Touchscreen:** Press a finger below the tiles and drag your finger right to left. Or swipe from right to left, lifting your finger quickly. To scroll left, drag or swipe your finger from left to right.

- **Keyboard:** Press the Page Down (PgDn) key to scroll to the right. Press Page Up (PgUp) to scroll to the left.

The Travel flash screen appears briefly. The Travel home screen appears, as shown in **Figure 2-4.**

8. Scroll to the right for an overview of the Travel app, which shows travel destinations, photos, and articles.

9. Switch to the Start screen using one of the methods in Step 3. Note that when you switch between Travel (or another app) and the Start screen, the Weather app remains hidden. Note as well that the live Travel tile shows changing destinations.

10. On the Start screen, select the Weather tile. Switch back and forth from the Weather app to the Start screen a few times to get comfortable switching between an app and the Start screen.

BING TRAVEL

San Francisco, California

Figure 2-4

Switch between Weather and Travel

1. Open the Weather app as in the preceding section.

2. Switch to the Start screen, and open the Travel app.

3. Switch directly between open apps (without going to the Start screen) by using one of these methods:

> • **Mouse:** Move the mouse pointer to the upper-left corner of the screen. A thumbnail preview of the Weather app appears in that corner, as shown in **Figure 2-5**. Click the left mouse button.

Travel thumbnail

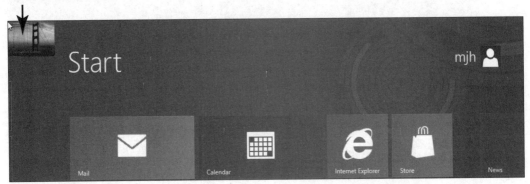

Figure 2-5

> If clicking in the left corner doesn't switch to the other app, you may not have two apps open. Or you may have more than two apps open, in which case you must click repeatedly until the desired app is displayed.

- **Touchscreen:** Press and hold down your finger outside the left edge of the screen. Drag your finger to the right and lift your finger when the other app appears. This action is called a *swipe*. It's kinda cool.

- **Keyboard:** Press ⊞+Tab. (In other words, while pressing and holding down the ⊞ key, press the Tab key. Then release both keys quickly.) The *app switcher* appears on the left and then the screen switches to the Weather app. You find out more about this feature next.

Use the App Switcher

1. Start the Weather app, and then start the Travel app.

2. Switch back to the Start screen.

3. Use one of the following methods to display the app switcher (see **Figure** 2-6), which shows thumbnails for open apps, and switch to the Weather app:

- **Mouse:** Place the pointer in the upper-left corner of the screen. Don't click. When a thumbnail appears, move the mouse pointer down until the app switcher appears. Click the Weather thumbnail.

- **Touchscreen:** Slowly swipe from the left edge of the screen, and then swipe back to the left edge without lifting your finger. Tap the Weather thumbnail.

- **Keyboard:** Hold down the ⊞ key, and press and release the Tab key to display the app switcher. Press Tab until the Weather thumbnail is highlighted. Then release both keys.

 When you quickly press and release both ⊞ and Tab, the app switcher appears briefly. When you instead hold down ⊞ and press and release Tab, the app switcher remains on the screen and you can keep pressing Tab to select different thumbnails. Release ⊞ to switch to the highlighted app. If you press ⊞+Ctrl+Tab — a test of your dexterity — the app switcher stays on-screen without you having to hold down any keys. Then you can press Tab to select the thumbnail you want and Enter or the space bar to switch to that app. (That may be more than you wanted to know, but it's literally handy.)

App switcher

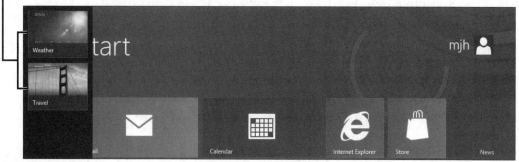

Figure 2-6

 In **Figure 2-6**, thumbnails appear for Weather and Travel apps. You may see the Start screen at the bottom of the app switcher, instead of one of the other apps. No thumbnail appears for the app you are using when you display the app switcher.

 You can switch between two apps without seeing the app switcher, as detailed in the preceding section. The app switcher comes in handy when you want to see thumbnails for several open apps at once.

Snap Two Apps to Display Both

1. From the Start screen, open the Weather and Travel apps, if they're not already open. (Refer to the "Open the Weather and Travel Apps" section.) Switch to the Travel app.

2. Use one of these techniques to *snap* (position) the Weather app next to the Travel app, as shown in **Figure 2-7**.

   • **Mouse:** Place the mouse pointer in the upper-left corner of the screen. Hold down the left mouse button and drag the Weather thumbnail down until the screen splits into a narrow pane on the left for the Weather app and a wider pane on the right for Travel. Release the mouse button.

- **Touchscreen:** Swipe (press your finger down and drag) from beyond the left edge of the screen to the right. When the Weather app thumbnail appears, drag just far enough to see the screen split. A quick swipe from the left replaces one app with another. A slow swipe splits the screen.

- **Keyboard:** Press ⊞ and the period key to snap the current app to one side. Press ⊞+period (.) again to snap to the other side. Use the app switcher to position the other app in the larger area of the screen. Press ⊞+period a third time to restore one app to full screen. You can continue repeating this sequence until you find the screen arrangement you prefer.

Divider   Dots

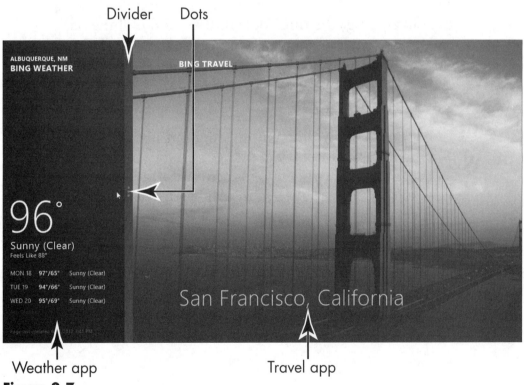

Weather app   Travel app

Figure 2-7

In the preceding section, you dragged an app far enough toward the middle of the screen to replace another app. To snap, don't drag the second app too far from the edge of the screen. Watch for the screen to split.

 If you can't get the two apps side-by-side, the problem may be your screen resolution, not you. The minimum screen resolution for side-by-side app display is 1366 pixels (dots) wide by 768 pixels high. If you can't complete these steps, your screen may not support this feature. See the book's website (www. win8mjh.com) for information on checking and changing screen resolution.

3. Give the Weather app the larger share of the screen by dragging the bar between the two apps or double-clicking (double-tapping) the three dots in the middle of the bar that separates the two panes (refer to **Figure 2-7**). The two windows are restricted in size, roughly 20 percent to 80 percent, as shown in **Figure 2-8**. You can't choose sizes in between.

 Apps may show different information or functions when snapped to the smaller pane. Note in the figure that only the Flight Status function is available in the narrower Travel pane. Similarly, when Weather is in the smaller pane, only the next few days are forecast.

4. Drag the bar between panes all the way left or right to make one app full screen.

5. If the Travel app isn't on-screen already, switch to it by using the app switcher (see the preceding section).

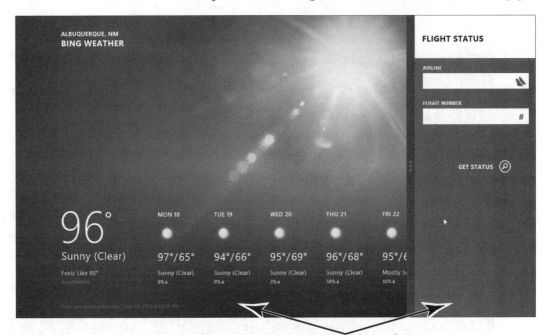

Reproportioned windows

Figure 2-8

6. Place Weather on the right instead of the left by dragging the Weather app thumbnail to the right side of the screen before letting go. Now Travel is in the wide pane on the left and Weather is in the narrow pane on the right, as shown in **Figure 2-9**. This procedure is different than resizing the two panes, as you did in Step 4 (refer to **Figure 2-7**), because Weather is on the right.

7. Drag the bar between the panes left or right far enough to hide one app, leaving the other full screen.

 To avoid snapping when you don't want two apps on screen at once, use the mouse to drag the incoming app thumbnail far enough to see its left edge. Watch how the screen changes between snap and full screen. Then let go of the thumbnail. With a touch-screen, a quick swipe or *flick* from the left replaces one app with another. A slow swipe splits the screen; to snap, let go when you see that split.

Figure 2-9

Close the Weather and Travel Apps

1. On the Start screen, select the Weather app tile. Switching to another app or the Start screen hides the Weather app but doesn't *close* it (stop it from running).

2. Close any open app with one of these methods:

- **Mouse:** Move the mouse pointer to the top edge of the screen, where the pointer changes to an open hand (see the margin). Hold down the left mouse button and the hand closes. Drag the app down to the bottom of the window. When part of the app is off the bottom of the screen, the app shrinks to a thumbnail. Let go to close the app.

- **Touchscreen:** Place your finger above the top edge of the screen (off the screen). Swipe down to the bottom of the window. When part of the app is off the bottom of the screen, the app shrinks to a thumbnail. Let go and the app closes.

- **Keyboard**: Press Alt+F4.

You don't have to close apps. However, having unneeded apps open makes switching between apps more of a challenge because of unneeded thumbnails in the app switcher.

3. On the Start screen again, select the Travel app tile.

4. In Travel, drag down or swipe down until the app shrinks and then let go to close the app. Or press Alt+F4.

You can use the mouse to close an app by using the app switcher. Position the pointer over a thumbnail and click with the right button. A context menu appears, as shown in **Figure 2-10**. With the left button, click Close. You can also use this menu to Snap Left or Snap Right.

Close or snap selected app

Figure 2-10

Use the App Bar

1. From the Start screen, open the Travel app.

2. The *app bar*, shown in **Figure 2-11,** contains functions specific to the current app. Display the app bar by using one of these methods:

- **Mouse:** With the pointer anywhere in the app, right-click (click the right mouse button).

- **Touchscreen:** Swipe down from the top or up from the bottom. Use a short swipe; don't swipe far enough to close the app.

- **Keyboard:** Press ⊞+Z.

App bar

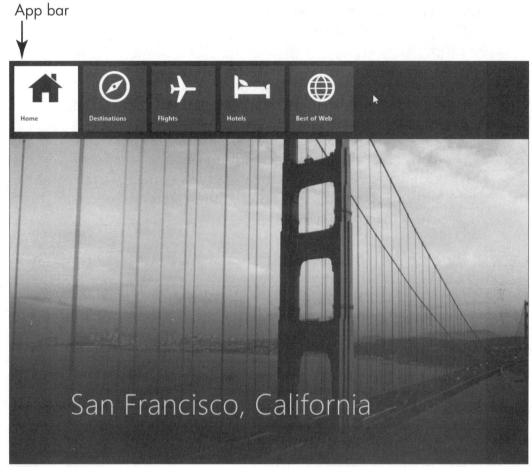

Figure 2-11

The app bar may appear across the bottom of the screen, the top of the screen, or in both locations.

3. In the Travel app, the app bar leads you to travel-specific functions. Select Destinations on the app bar, which then disappears. On the Destinations screen, scroll to the right for an overview. To refine the scope of your browsing, use the Region option.

4. Display the app bar in Travel again. Then select the Flights or Hotels button. You could use either in booking a trip.

5. Display the app bar again. Select the Home button to return to the app *home screen*, which is the screen you see when you start an app for the first time.

 You can also use the Back button (an arrow in a circle), which is found in the upper-left corner of many screens, to return to the preceding screen, not necessarily the home screen.

Add a Location in Weather

1. From the Start screen, open the Weather app. With the Weather app on the screen, display the app bar using one of the methods in the preceding section. In **Figure 2-12**, the Weather app bar appears at the top and bottom of the screen.

2. Select the Places button at the top of the screen. The Places screen appears, as shown in **Figure 2-13**. Unless you're lucky enough to live in Albuquerque, your screen will show a different live tile.

3. Select the Add Place tile, which looks like a plus in a circle. The Enter location screen appears.

4. Type a location name, such as a city, in the box under Enter Location, as shown in **Figure 2-14**. As you type, matching location names appear below the box. If you see the location you want, select that name to add a tile for that location to the Places screen. No need to click

the Add button, unless your location does not appear automatically.

 You can add other locations by repeating Steps 3 and 4.

App bar

App bar

Figure 2-12

Back arrow

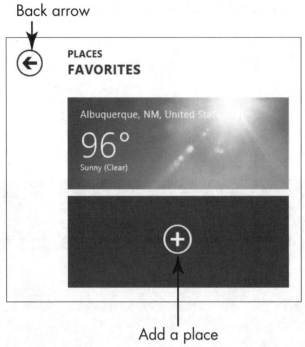

PLACES
FAVORITES

Albuquerque, NM, United State

96°
Sunny (Clear)

Add a place

Figure 2-13

Type in the box

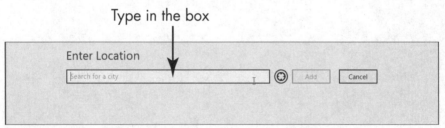

Enter Location

Search for a city   Add   Cancel

Figure 2-14

5. Select the tile for the location you added. The Weather app displays full information for the location you selected.

You can switch between multiple locations by using the Places button on the app bar.

6. Return to the Start screen. Your new location does not appear — yet. Select the Weather tile, and your added location appears. Display the app bar (see **Figure 2-15**). In addition to the app bar at the top of the screen, an app bar for the selected location appears at the bottom of the screen.

App bar
↓

App bar for the selected location
Figure 2-15

7. Select the Pin button at the bottom of the screen to add a tile for the current location to the Start screen. (If you don't see Pin, repeat Steps 2—5 to add a location.) You can add a note to the tile by selecting the X in the box where the location name appears, as shown in **Figure 2-16**, which clears the contents. Then, type your note. (For example, you might type a person's name if you display the weather where that person lives.) Then select the Pin to Start button.

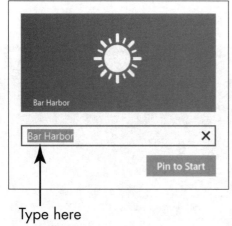

Type here

Figure 2-16

8. Return to the Start screen. The original Weather tile appears, as well as the new tile. You may have to scroll to the right with the mouse or by dragging your finger right to left to see the new Weather tile, as in **Figure 2-17**.

9. Select the new Weather tile to open the app with that location.

10. Display the app bar for Weather, which is shown in **Figure 2-18**. Select the Unpin button at the bottom of the screen to remove from the Start screen the tile for the current location. If Unpin doesn't appear, repeat Step 7.

Figure 2-17

Select the Unpin button
Figure 2-18

11. Return to the Start screen. The location you unpinned no longer appears.

 Add locations for friends, family, and travel destinations and pin these new locations to the Start screen. See the section "Arrange Apps on the Start Screen" if you want to group these tiles.

12. In the Weather app, several other buttons may appear. See if your screen displays any of the following (refer to **Figure 2-18**):

- The Home button (on the top app bar) displays weather for the *default* (original) location if you are displaying any other location.

- The World Weather button (on the top app bar) is cool. Select it now! A map of the world appears with weather for some locations. Click or tap an area on the map to zoom in for more locations. Select any location to display weather full-screen for that location. (This action does not add the location to your list of places.) Select the Back button if you want to return to the main Weather screen without displaying a new location.

- The Set as Default button (on the bottom app bar) makes the currently displayed location the default location (or Home).

- The Add button (on the bottom app bar but not shown in **Figure 2-18**) appears for a location you chose from World Weather. Use the Add button if you want to add the displayed location to the Places screen.

- The Remove button appears for a location you have added. Use the Remove button to unclutter the Places screen.

- The Change to Celsius button switches temperatures to that scale, in which case the button becomes Change to Fahrenheit.

- The Refresh button updates the screen, although that should happen automatically.

Change App Settings

1. On the Start screen, select the Weather tile.

2. In the Weather app, display the charms bar and select the Settings charm using one of the following methods:

- **Mouse:** Move the pointer to the lower-right corner of the screen to display the charms bar. Click the Settings charm.

- **Touchscreen:** Swipe from the right edge toward the left. Tap Settings.

- **Keyboard:** Press ⊞+I to display the Settings panel without displaying the charms bar first. This shortcut key is hard to beat for quick access to Settings.

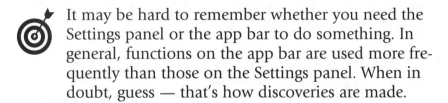 It may be hard to remember whether you need the Settings panel or the app bar to do something. In general, functions on the app bar are used more frequently than those on the Settings panel. When in doubt, guess — that's how discoveries are made.

3. The Settings panel for Weather appears, as shown in **Figure 2-19**. Select each of the following settings in Weather. Use the Back button (the back arrow) to move from each of these back to the main Settings panel.

Figure 2-19

- The Options setting displays a screen that includes Search History, which records searches you make in the Weather app for locations (see the preceding section). The Clear History button erases any previous location searches, but not locations you added or pinned. Leave the Search History settings as they are for now.

- The About option displays the app's version number and creator along with additional information.

- The Image Credits option credits the photographers who took the terrific pictures used in the Weather app.

- Use the Feedback option to provide direct feed-back to the app developer, which in this case is Microsoft. See **Figure 2-20**. Your comments may help improve the app.

- The Terms of Use and Privacy Statement options open in the browser web pages with specific legal language regarding the app. In general, you have no rights and they have no liabilities.

- The Permissions option also displays version infor-mation and privacy settings. Turn on the Location function to enable the Weather app to access your location automatically based on your network. (You probably did this the first time you opened Weather.) This feature is useful if you take your computer to other cities. Turn off the Location function to control the location manually. The Lock Screen option controls whether or not the app runs in the background and appears on the Lock screen. Turn it on.

- The Rate and Review option opens the Microsoft Store. See Chapter 9 for information about using the Microsoft Store and reviewing apps.

 The top portion of the Settings panel is specific to the open app. The bottom section contains systemwide settings, covered in Chapters 3 and 4.

 Changes to settings take effect immediately. You don't have to save or activate your changes.

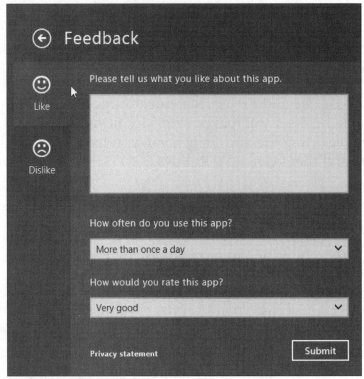

Figure 2-20

Search for the Calculator Desktop App

1. On the Start screen, begin to type the word *calculator*. The Search panel appears on the right side of the screen, as shown in **Figure 2-21**, with the letters you type appearing in a box in the upper right of the screen. On the left, apps beginning with those letters appear. When you see the Calculator tile on the left, select it.

 You can search for more than apps, including settings and files. To use Search in any app, display the charms bar and select the Search charm. For example, search for a city in the Weather or Travel apps.

2. The Calculator app opens on the desktop, as shown in **Figure 2-22**. To perform a calculation, select the buttons on the screen or use a keyboard.

Search text

Figure 2-21

Calculator tile   Desktop

Figure 2-22

3. Return to the Start screen: Click in the lower-left corner of the desktop, or swipe in from the left edge of the screen, or press ⊞.

4. Repeat the steps you just used to switch back and forth between the Start screen and the Calculator app on the desktop.

5. Switch to the Start screen.

6. Display the app switcher and switch back to the desktop using one of the following methods:

- **Mouse:** Move the pointer to the upper-left corner to reveal the desktop thumbnail. Move the pointer down the left side of the screen without clicking to display the app switcher. Drag the desktop thumbnail to the right; drag a little to split the screen or more to fill the screen.

- **Touchscreen:** Swipe from the left edge of the screen and back to display the app switcher. Swipe the desktop thumbnail to the right slowly to split the screen or quickly to fill the screen.

- **Keyboard:** Press ⊞+Tab until the desktop thumbnail is highlighted, then release both keys.

 You can use two keystrokes to switch to desktop apps. Press Alt+Tab to display thumbnails for open Windows 8 apps, open desktop apps, and the desktop itself. Press ⊞+D to switch from the Start screen to the desktop. See Chapter 5 for more information on the desktop.

 If your screen resolution allows, you can snap the desktop beside other apps. This procedure works best when the desktop is in the larger part of the screen. Note that you can snap only the entire desktop, not individual desktop apps.

7. Close the entire desktop like any other app, with one of the following methods:

- **Mouse:** Move the mouse pointer to the top center of the desktop until the pointer changes into an open hand. Drag down until part of the desktop is off the screen, and then release the mouse button to close the desktop.

- **Touchscreen:** Swipe down from the top edge until part of the desktop is off the screen.

 These methods close both the Calculator and the desktop. To close only the Calculator, switch to the desktop and click the white X in the red box in the upper-right corner of the Calculator (refer to **Figure 2-22**).

Display All Windows 8 Apps

1. The Start screen displays only some of the apps available in Windows 8. To see all the apps in Windows 8, display the app bar for the Start screen (see **Figure 2-23)** and select the All Apps button using one of these methods:

- **Mouse:** Move the mouse pointer away from the tiles and other on-screen objects and then right-click. The app bar for the Start screen appears across the bottom of the screen. In the app bar, click the All Apps button.

- **Touchscreen:** Swipe up from the bottom edge of the screen or down from the top edge to display the app bar. Tap the All Apps button.

- **Keyboard:** Press ⊞+Z, and then press Enter.

App bar

Figure 2-23

2. The All Apps screen appears as shown in **Figure** 2-24.
You may have to roll the mouse wheel toward you or
drag from right to left to see all the icons. The apps are in
alphabetical order within groups, some of which are
named:

- **Windows 8 apps:** Appear first in the list, without a
  heading. These apps run full screen and can be
  snapped side-by-side (if your computer supports
  the snap feature).

- **Windows Accessories apps:** Consist of desktop
  apps, such as Calculator. See Chapter 5 for information about using the desktop.

- **Windows Ease of Access apps:** Increase on-screen visibility, read text aloud from the screen, enable voice commands and dictation, and display an on-screen keyboard. See Chapter 3 for more information.

- **Windows System apps:** Consist of computer management tools, some of which are covered in Part IV.

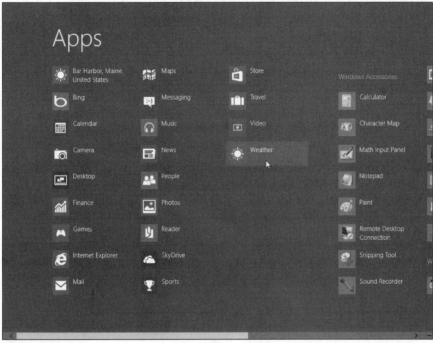

Figure 2-24

 You may see other groups for programs on your system.

3. Open one of your old standby apps: Weather, Travel, or Calculator.

4. Return to the Start screen.

Arrange Apps on the Start Screen

1. Search for the Calculator app (see the "Search for the Calculator Desktop App" section).

2. On the Search results screen, use one of the following methods to select — but not open — the Calculator tile, shown in **Figure 2-25**:

   - **Mouse:** Position the pointer over the Calculator tile and right-click (a left click would open the Calculator).

   - **Touchscreen:** Swipe slightly down or up on the Calculator tile (a direct tap would open Calculator).

   - **Keyboard:** Use the arrow keys to select Calculator. Then press the context menu key (shown in the margin), which is usually next to the right-hand ⊞ key.

    A check mark next to a tile indicates that the tile is selected.

3. The app bar appears automatically when you select a tile. Select Pin to Start. The app bar disappears.

4. On the same screen (refer to **Figure 2-25**), select the Calculator tile again. Note that the Unpin from Start option replaces Pin to Start in the preceding step. In the future, use Unpin from Start to remove tiles you don't want on the Start screen. (The programs are not removed when you unpin.)

The app is selected

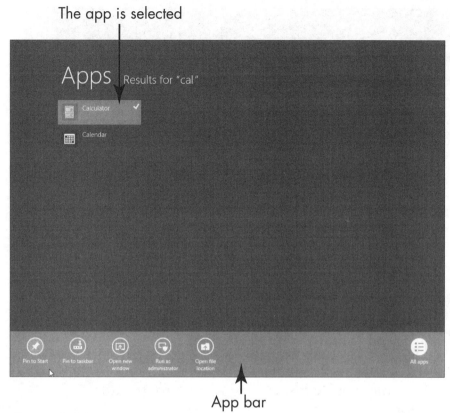

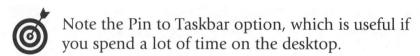

App bar

Figure 2-25

Note the Pin to Taskbar option, which is useful if you spend a lot of time on the desktop.

5. Return to the Start screen. In **Figure 2-26**, the Calculator tile appears at the right end of the apps. You may have to roll the mouse wheel or drag the screen to see the Calculator tile.

Figure 2-26

6. Drag the Calculator tile to a new location. As you move the tile, other tiles move out of the way, like a game of Dodge Tile.

7. Create a new group for Calculator by dragging the Calculator tile to the right of all the other tiles. When a vertical bar appears, as shown in **Figure 2-27,** release the Calculator tile. You've just created a new group with Calculator as the only tile.

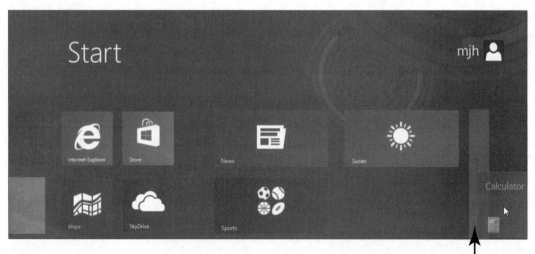

Drag until the bar appears

Figure 2-27

8. It's time to name the new group. Begin by *zooming* out:

- **Mouse:** Move the pointer into the lower-right corner of the screen and click the tiny magnifying lens. Or press down the Ctrl key as you roll the mouse wheel toward you.

- **Touchscreen:** Place two fingers on the screen and *pinch* — slowly move your fingers together.

 Instead of two fingers on one hand, you can use one finger from each hand to pinch.

- **Keyboard:** Press Ctrl+minus to zoom out.

The Start screen zooms out to show all icons (refer to **Figure 2-27**). This zoomed-out screen is different from the screen that shows all your apps (refer to **Figure 2-24**).

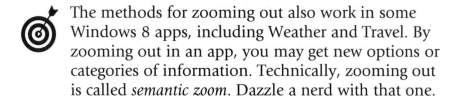 The methods for zooming out also work in some Windows 8 apps, including Weather and Travel. By zooming out in an app, you may get new options or categories of information. Technically, zooming out is called *semantic zoom*. Dazzle a nerd with that one.

9. Select the Calculator's group and display the app bar as in **Figure 2-28** by putting the pointer over the group and right-clicking or by dragging the group up or down slightly.

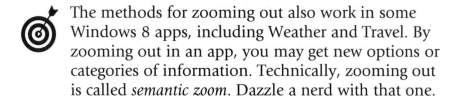 A check mark on the group indicates that the group is selected. Note that the Calculator group is so small that the check mark covers the Calculator tile in **Figure 2-28**.

Select a group to name

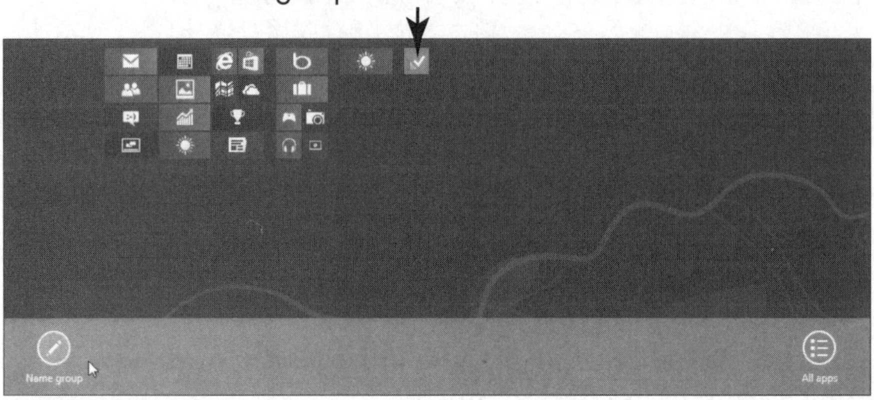

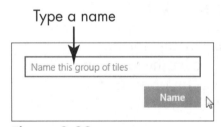

Figure 2-28

10. In the app bar, select Name Group. In the pop-up window that appears, as shown in **Figure 2-29,** type a name for the group and then select the Name button. The new name appears above the group in the zoomed display, although the name may appear shortened on this screen. You can change the name at any time by repeating these steps. To remove the name, select the X to the right of the text box.

Type a name

Name this group of tiles

Name

Figure 2-29

11. On the zoomed screen, move your new group to the left of the others by dragging the group. As you move the group, other groups move out of the way. Dodge Group!

12. Return to the Start screen and check out the new group's location and name (see **Figure 2-30**). You're in control.

Figure 2-30

 The Start menu becomes more useful and personal when you eliminate tiles you don't need and arrange tiles to suit your sense of order.

Adjusting Windows 8 PC Settings

*O*ut of the box, Windows 8 is showy and colorful. If you don't like that look, however, you can change the photos and colors you see on the screen. Adjusting Windows 8 PC settings can also make Windows 8 easier and more fun to use. When you're ready, you can dive in and make Windows 8 yours.

In this chapter, you personalize the Lock screen and change the colors and background design on the Start screen. You'll see these screens many times a day, so they should please you. Choose a picture to identify your account. Finally, make your screen easier to see and enable features such as Narrator, which reads aloud content from the screen.

Many people leave Windows 8 largely as they found it. Some love to tweak, tinker, and tune. How far you go in personalizing Windows 8 is up to you — it's your computer, after all.

 See Chapter 4 for information on changing passwords and other User settings.

Access PC Settings

1. On the Start screen, display the charms bar (see **Figure** 3-1) and select Settings with one of these methods:

- **Mouse:** Move the mouse pointer into the lower-right corner of the screen to display the charms bar, and then click Settings.

- **Touchscreen:** Swipe from the right edge of the screen to display the charms bar, and then tap Settings.

- **Keyboard:** Press ▦+I to go straight to Settings, skipping the charms bar.

 You can complete the following steps with a mouse, the keyboard, or a touchscreen. Find the right combination of methods for you. Experiment and play.

2. The Settings panel appears, the bottom portion of which is shown in **Figure** 3-2. Select Change PC Settings by moving the pointer over the item and clicking, or by tapping the item.

 Options near the top of the Settings panel are for the open app, if any.

3. The PC Settings screen appears, as shown in **Figure** 3-3. One at a time, select each heading on the left, starting with Personalize, to see the options available. In this chapter, you focus mainly on the Personalize settings.

Settings charm

Figure 3-1

Select to view the PC Settings screen

Figure 3-2

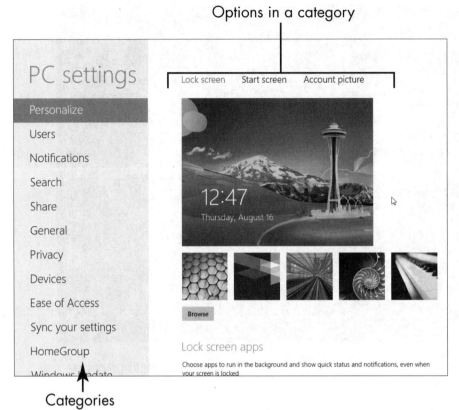

Options in a category

Categories

Figure 3-3

Personalize the Lock Screen

1. On the PC Settings screen, select Personalize (refer to **Figure** 3-3).

2. At the top of the screen, select Lock Screen. **Figure 3-3** shows the current Lock screen.

The Lock screen is the first screen you see when you start Windows 8.

3. Just above the Browse button, select each thumbnail photo, one at a time. The larger preview photo above changes and the thumbnails shift to the right, with the previously selected photo taking the first position in the row, as shown in **Figure** 3-4. Select a photo that's different from the one you started with. (You can always change it later.)

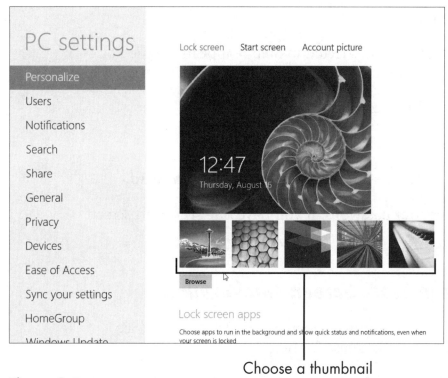

Choose a thumbnail

Figure 3-4

 You can use the Browse button to select one of your own photos from the Pictures library. See Chapter 10 for information on adding photos to your library.

4. Return to the Start screen. Select your account name in the upper-right corner to display the menu shown in **Figure** 3-5, and then select Lock to display the Lock screen.

 You can lock your computer anytime by pressing ⊞+L.

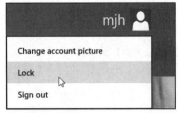

Figure 3-5

5. The photo you selected in Step 3 appears on the Lock screen. Display the Password screen as follows:

- **Mouse:** Click anywhere.

- **Touchscreen:** Swipe up.

- **Keyboard:** Press any key on the keyboard.

6. Enter your password, if you have one. The Start screen appears.

Change the Start Screen Background

1. On the PC Settings screen, select Personalize. (See "Access PC Settings" for help.)

2. At the top of the screen, select Start Screen. You see a preview of the color and background of the Start screen, as shown in **Figure 3-6**.

   You will see the Start screen more often than any other screen, so personalize it to make it yours.

3. Using a click or a tap, select a background pattern thumbnail from those below the larger preview. Your selection appears in the preview area.

   If you'd like a solid color background, with no design behind the tiles, select the last thumbnail in the bottom row.

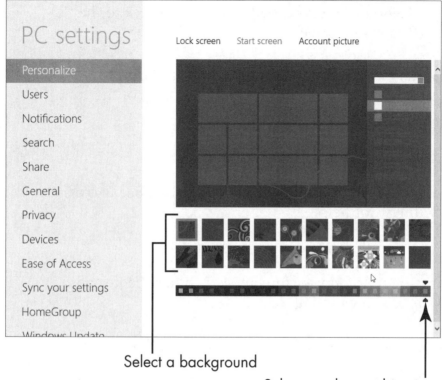

Select a background

Select a color combination

Figure 3-6

4. Using a click or a tap, select a color combination from the row of colors below the thumbnails. The color of the PC Settings heading and the background color of the Personalize heading change immediately. Try a different color.

5. To see the effect on the Start screen, switch to that screen as follows:

- **Mouse:** Click the pointer in the lower-left corner of the screen. Repeat to switch back to the Personalize screen.

- **Touchscreen:** Swipe from the right edge to display the charms bar, and then tap the Start charm. Repeat to switch back to the Personalize screen.

- **Keyboard:** Press ⊞. Repeat to switch back to the Personalize screen.

 It may seem illogical that repeating an action switches back and forth (*toggles*), but each of these actions does.

Choose an Account Picture

1. On the PC Settings screen, select Personalize. See "Access PC Settings" for help.

2. At the top of the screen, select Account Picture.

3. Your current Account picture appears. It may be just an outline, as shown in **Figure** 3-7.

Current account picture

Figure 3-7

Your account picture appears on the password screen and on the Start screen.

4. To choose one of your photos, select the Browse button. The file picker appears. Select a photo and then select the Choose Image button. Or select Cancel to return to the previous screen without changing your account picture.

See Chapter 10 for information about adding photos to your Pictures library.

5. If you have a built-in or attached camera (called a *webcam*), select the Camera app under Create an Account Picture. The Camera app opens with a preview of what your camera sees. If you see Connect a Camera, select the back arrow to the left of Camera. See Chapter 10 for information on taking pictures with a webcam.

You may be able to use another app to select or create a picture. Select the app under Create an Account Picture (refer to **Figure 3-7**).

6. Return to the Start screen to see your new account picture (mine is shown in **Figure 3-8** — a photo of Luke the Lovehound by Merri Rudd) using one of these methods:

- **Mouse:** Click the pointer in the lower-left corner of the screen. Repeat to switch back to the Personalize screen.

- **Touchscreen:** Swipe from the right edge of the screen and then tap the Start button. Repeat to switch back to the Personalize screen.

- **Keyboard:** Press ⊞. Repeat to switch back to the Personalize screen.

The easiest way to access the Personalize settings is through your account name. In the upper-right corner of the Start screen, select your name and then select Change Account Picture. Voila! The PC Settings screen appears, with Personalize selected. You don't have to change your picture to use this shortcut to PC Settings.

Change your account picture

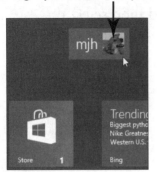

Figure 3-8

Make Windows 8 Easier to Use

1. On the PC Settings screen, select Ease of Access, as shown in **Figure** 3-9. (See "Access PC Settings" for help.)

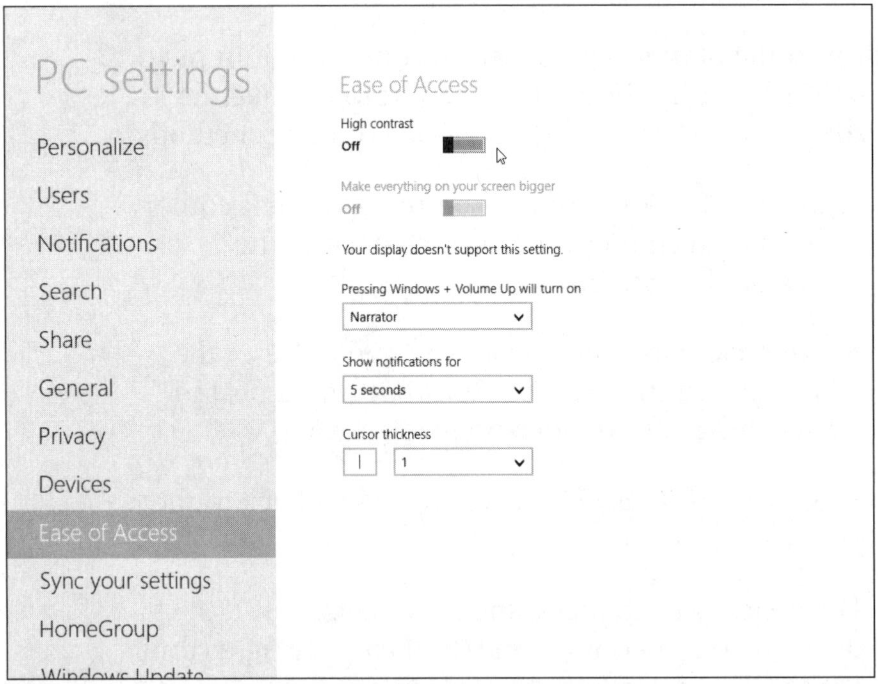

Figure 3-9

2. To alter the screen in a way that might make it easier to see text, select anywhere in the rectangle under High Contrast to turn on that feature. This rectangle mimics a switch, indicating off (a square to the left in the rectangle) or on (a square to the right). The screen displays a brief *Please wait* message and the screen shown in **Figure 3-10** appears. As you can see, the On setting changes screen text and objects from black to white and changes the background to black. The background of selected text and some objects appears in blue.

Choose High Contrast for white on black

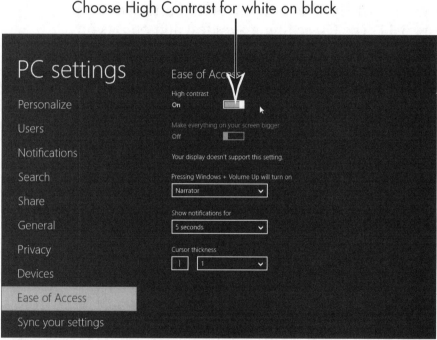

Figure 3-10

 The colors displayed by the High Contrast option were chosen because Microsoft considers them a suitable alternative to standard black text on a white background. You can't adjust these colors.

With High Contrast on, selecting the Personalize category displays *You are currently in High Contrast, which disables some personalization settings.* To re-enable those personalization settings, such as background color, turn off the High Contrast option.

3. If you want to turn off High Contrast, select the rectangle again, to the left side this time.

4. Select the rectangle under Make Everything on Your Screen Bigger. (Your screen may not support this option, in which case you'll see a message like the one in **Figure** 3-9.) The change to the screen is shown in **Figure 3-11.** The On setting makes text and objects on the screen bigger than normal, making it easier to see a portion of the screen. However, less content fits on the screen at one time, so you must move the screen more. If the PC Settings categories are now off-screen, use the back arrow next to Ease of Access to see them.

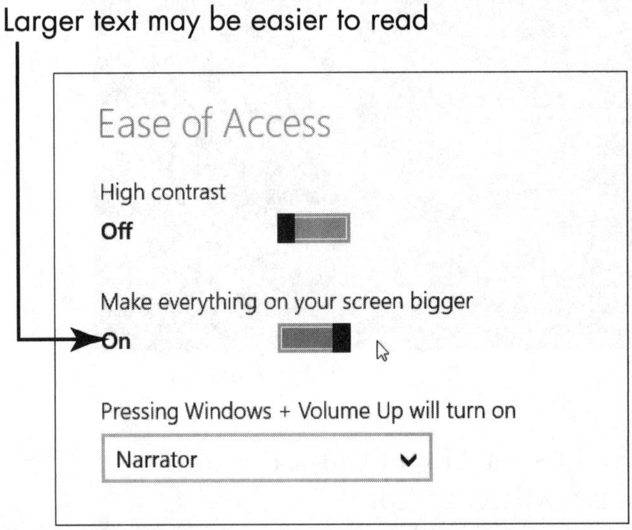

Larger text may be easier to read

Ease of Access

High contrast
Off

Make everything on your screen bigger
On

Pressing Windows + Volume Up will turn on

Narrator ⌄

Figure 3-11

5. If you want to turn off the Make Everything on Your Screen Bigger setting, select the rectangle again, to the left side this time.

6. The option Pressing Windows + Volume Up Will Turn On determines what happens when you press and hold down the Windows (⊞) key as you press the volume up button, which is found on the edge of most tablets and along the top or side of some keyboards (look for a conical speaker icon with + or multiple curved lines). Under the option, select the rectangle and then select one of these choices:

- **Nothing** does what it says.

- **Magnifier** zooms a portion of the screen for easier viewing, as shown in **Figure 3-12.** Text and objects will be larger than they are with the Make Everything on Your Screen Bigger option. Drag the screen to see other areas. Select the on-screen magnifying lens to change settings or to close Magnifier.

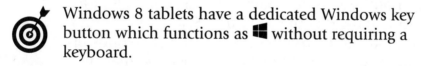

   Windows 8 tablets have a dedicated Windows key button which functions as ⊞ without requiring a keyboard.

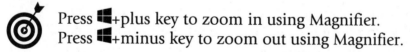

   Press ⊞+plus key to zoom in using Magnifier. Press ⊞+minus key to zoom out using Magnifier.

- **Narrator** reads aloud content on the screen.

- **On-Screen Keyboard** enables typing without using a physical keyboard. This on-screen keyboard uses the layout of a conventional keyboard. However, most people find that the standard Windows 8 virtual keyboard is more flexible. See Chapter 1 for information on the virtual keyboard layouts.

Don't drag the magnifier icon; use it to change the settings

Figure 3-12

7. The Show Notifications For setting controls how long certain pop-up messages appear before disappearing. These notifications are sometimes called *tooltips* or *toasts* (because of the way they pop up). Select the box under this option and then select the number of seconds or minutes you want notifications to linger on the screen. By default, notifications disappear after 5 seconds, which usually isn't enough time to read a long notification. Note that notifications disappear when you move the mouse or select another option.

 I suggest that you try 30 seconds for the delay.

8. To check out your new notifications setting, position the mouse pointer in the lower-right corner until you see the Settings panel. Then move the pointer up and click Settings.

 This step works only with a mouse, although you will see notifications in other places without using a mouse.

Place the mouse pointer over the keyboard icon to the right of Power. In **Figure 3-13**, a notification pops up identifying the current language and keyboard settings. Click anywhere in the PC Settings screen to dismiss the Settings panel.

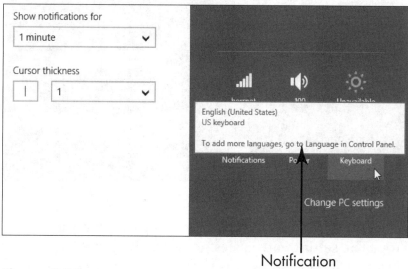

Notification

Figure 3-13

9. Cursor Thickness, the last setting on the Ease of Access panel, controls the width of the vertical blinking line that appears when you can type text. The box on the left under this heading displays the current cursor (without blinking). The default thickness is 1 pixel, which is a thin line. To try a different thickness, select a number in the box to the right. (You might try a cursor thickness of 2 or 3 pixels.)

10. To see the new cursor in action, switch to the Start screen and type any text to begin searching. The box in the top-right corner of the screen displays the cursor along with your text. **Figure 3-14** shows a cursor 4 pixels thick.

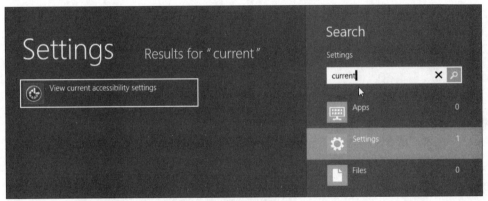

Figure 3-14

 More Ease of Access settings are available through the desktop. The settings are easiest to access by pressing ⊞+U (for *usability*). Another way to access them is to type *current* on the Start screen, select Settings on the right, and then select the View Current Accessibility Settings tile on the left. The screen switches to the Ease of Access Center on the desktop, as shown in **Figure 3-15.** See Chapter 5 for more information about using the desktop.

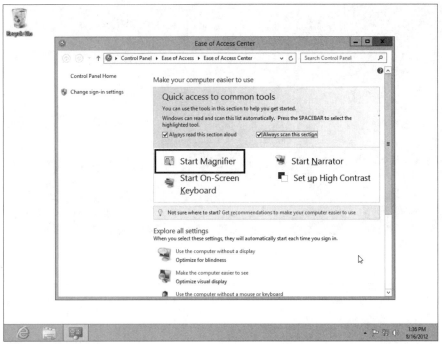

Figure 3-15

Check for Important Updates

1. To check for updates to Windows 8, type **update** on the Start screen. On the search results screen, select Settings, as shown in **Figure 3-16,** and then select Windows Update.

> If you don't mind typing, searching for Windows Update is more direct than stepping through Charms⇨Settings⇨Change PC Settings⇨Windows Update.

2. The Windows Update screen informs you that Windows 8 automatically installs important updates, such as security enhancements. You also see when Windows 8 last checked for updates and whether any were found. Select the Check for Updates Now button, shown in **Figure 3-17.**

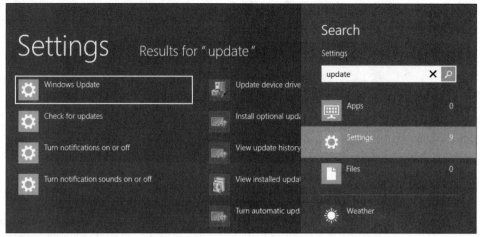

Figure 3-16

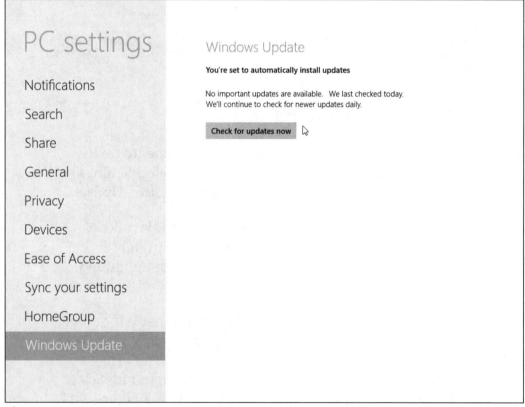

Figure 3-17

3. You may see a message that one or more updates have been scheduled to be installed. You do not have to do anything to install these updates — the update process is automatic. However, if you select the link to schedule updates, you can see details and select the Install button if you want to. Otherwise, return to the Start screen to let Windows 8 manage updates automatically.

 Installing an update seldom takes more than a few minutes. You can use your system during the update process. If the update process requires that you restart your computer, you will see a message on the Windows Update screen and the Lock screen. If you don't restart when required, Windows 8 will automatically restart within two days of the first notification.

 For information on other updates and maintaining Windows 8, see Chapter 12.

Working with User Accounts

Windows 8 seeks out an Internet connection automatically from the moment you start it. More often than not, you connect to the Internet using a wireless or *Wi-Fi* connection. For this reason, if you start a laptop or tablet in a coffee shop or library, you may see a notification that one or more network connections are available. That's convenient.

A computer without an Internet connection is an island, if not a paperweight. Connecting to a network, however, opens a door to your computer — and malefactors try to push through that door to access your computer. Windows 8 has a *firewall* that monitors and restricts traffic in and out. Don't be afraid of connecting to the Internet, but be aware of the risks and be careful to which networks you connect. In Chapter 1, you create a local user account. You need a Microsoft Account to take full advantage of Windows 8 features such as the Microsoft Store for apps (see Chapter 9), SkyDrive for online storage, and synchronizing settings between computers. In this chapter, you create a Microsoft Account and choose a secure method for logging into your account. To control access to your computer, you find out how to use a password, a shorter personal identification number (*PIN*), or even a personal photo to unlock your computer.

Get ready to . . .

Microsoft uses an e-mail address to identify your account. You can use any existing e-mail address or create an e-mail address as part of setting up your account. Each is covered in a separate section.

If other people use your computer, you may want to create more than one user account. If each person who uses the computer has a separate account, you can keep data, apps, and settings tidy and private.

Even if you're the only one using your computer, you may want more than one account. For example, if you create a new local user account, you can experiment with the new account — changing the look and function of Windows 8 — without affecting your first account.

 Many of the steps in this chapter involve entering text, such as your name. If you don't have a physical keyboard, use the virtual keyboard, which is covered in Chapter 1.

Connect to the Internet

1. On the Start screen, display the charms bar (shown in **Figure** 4-1) using one of these methods:

   • **Mouse:** Place the mouse pointer in the lower-right corner of the screen and move the pointer up.

   • **Touchscreen:** Drag your finger from the right edge of the screen to the left.

   • **Keyboard:** Press ⊞+C.

2. To the left of the time and date is a network connection icon. Refer to Table 4-1 to determine which network connection icon appears on your screen.

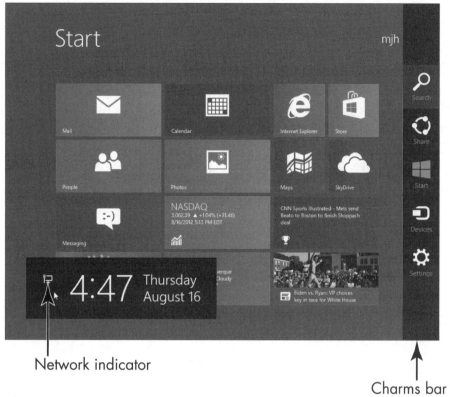

Network indicator

Charms bar

Figure 4-1

Table 4-1	Network Connection Icons
Icon	***What It Means***
	You aren't connected but wireless (Wi-Fi) connections are available. The more solid bars, the stronger the connection.
	A wireless connection has been established.
	A wired connection has been established. Your computer is plugged into a router, a device that connects to the phone company's DSL or to cable TV.
	You have no current connection and no available connections. (The x can appear over a plug, as it does here, or over bars.)

3. Select the Settings charm. In the Settings panel on the right, you see the network connection icon again. The Network icon indicates information about the current network connection, if any (refer to Table 4-1). The icon itself will indicate whether the connection is wired (a plug) or wireless (five bars). Under the icon, you may see one of the following:

- **Network name:** If you are connected to a wired or wireless network, the name of the network will appear below the icon. In that case, you're all set, but keep reading.

- *Available:* A wireless connection that you may be able to connect to is available.

- *Unavailable:* No connection has been established or is available.

 Select or choose options by moving the mouse pointer and left-clicking or by tapping a touchscreen with your finger.

4. Select the Network icon. The Networks panel appears, as shown in **Figure 4-2,** and lists all available network connections. There may be no connections or dozens.

Available wireless connections

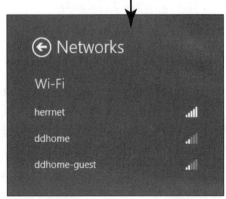

Figure 4-2

If you see *Not connected* and *No connections available,* you may be out of luck. Check your computer documentation to see whether your PC has wireless capability and whether you need to turn on a mechanical switch. The Troubleshoot button on the screen opens Help on the desktop. See Chapter 5 for information on using the desktop.

 If your computer is near a router (DSL or cable) and you don't have wireless capability, connect your PC and the router using an Ethernet cable, which is thicker than a phone line, with wider connections. Ethernet cables may be yellow or green.

5. Select a connection. Note that not all displayed connections are accessible or desirable.

 If you're not sure you can trust a connection, you might want to forego a connection — better safe than sorry. (Unsafe wireless connections can be used to eavesdrop on your activities, though that scenario is rare.) However, if an available connection sports the name of the establishment you're in or near, such as a restaurant or a coffee shop, the connection may be safe. The same is true of connections at libraries, airports, and many other public spaces.

 Generally, you want to select the connection with the strongest signal (most white bars). In addition, consider the connection speed. Hover the mouse pointer over a network tile, and you may see Type: 802.11, which is the general standard for wireless (Wi-Fi) connections. A letter at the end of that number indicates a slower connection (g) or faster one (n). If two connections are otherwise identical, (n) is preferable.

6. After you select a connection, the selected tile expands and displays the Connect Automatically check box, as shown in **Figure 4-3**. If you trust the connection and might want to use it again, leave the check box selected. Otherwise, deselect the check box. To continue, select the Connect button.

Connect automatically the next time

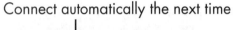

Figure 4-3

7. You may be prompted to enter a network security key (a series of characters), which limits access to those who know the key. See **Figure 4-4**. The key protects that network and its users. If you're using a hotel's connection, you can obtain the key from the front desk. If you don't know the key, select Cancel. Otherwise, enter the key (dots appear as you type) and select Next.

If the connection is public and open, you won't be prompted for a key. Open connections are common in libraries, coffee shops, and other places many people come and go.

A secure network requires a key

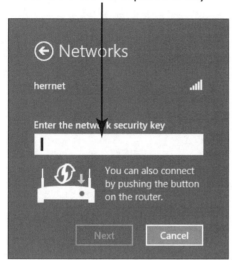

Figure 4-4

 If you have access to your *router*, which is a kind of network device connected to the phone line or cable TV, the router may have a button you can push to connect without using the security key (refer to the diagram in **Figure** 4-4).

8. If you entered the correct key or none was required, you may see the message shown in **Figure** 4-5: *Do you want to turn on sharing between PCs and connect to devices on this network? Sharing* refers to allowing computers access to your files or to a device, such as a printer. You should share at home but not in a public location. Choose one of the following:

- **No:** This option prevents you from connecting directly with other computers and protects your computer from networks in public places. You'll still have Internet access.

- **Yes:** This option enables you to share documents and devices between your computers on a home or office network.

Say "yes" at home but "no" in public

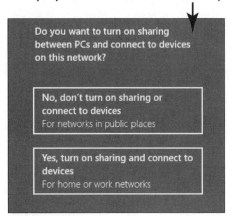

Figure 4-5

 If you're not sure about which option to choose, go with No.

9. When a Wi-Fi connection is established, *Connected* appears next to the network name in the Networks panel (**Figure** 4-6, left). Select the back arrow. The connection name and signal strength appear in the Settings panel (**Figure** 4-6, middle). Now display the charms bar (see Step 1 for help). The connection strength (but not the name) appears next to the time and date (**Figure** 4-6, right).

  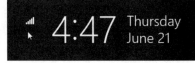

Figure 4-6

If you selected the Connect Automatically check box (in Step 6), the connection will be used anytime it is available. If you move your computer to another location out of range of this network (usually a few hundred yards), you will have to repeat these steps to connect to another network.

10. To turn off or disconnect the network connection, display the Networks panel again (Steps 1—4). Select the connected network (see **Figure 4-7**) and then select the Disconnect button. (If you disconnect this network, reconnect before continuing.)

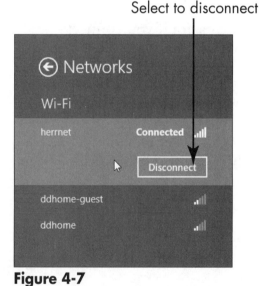

Figure 4-7

 Most of the time, you'll stay connected. When you shut down the computer or move the computer far enough away from the connection, it disconnects automatically.

11. In the Networks panel, right-click or tap, hold a moment, and then release to display a pop-up menu of functions related to the selected network, including the following:

- **Show Estimated Data Usage** is the most interesting of these functions, showing how much data has moved through the connection over time. This information is particularly important if you pay separately for data connections, as with some cell phone or mobile connections.

- **Set as Metered Connection** lets you put a limit on data transfer, which is useful if your bill is based on the amount of data you transfer.

- **Forget This Network** may be useful if you connect accidentally to a network or you want to practice connecting all over again.

- **Turn Sharing On or Off** switches to the desktop, where you can choose No, Don't or you can choose Yes, Turn on Sharing and Connect to Devices. You need this only if you think you made the wrong choice in Step 8.

- **View Connection Properties** switches to the desktop for more technical options. You're not likely to need this function.

Create a New E-Mail Address for a Microsoft Account

1. Follow these steps to switch your Windows 8 user account from local to a Microsoft Account with a new e-mail address. On the Start screen, select your name in the upper-right corner of the screen. In the pop-up menu that appears (see **Figure 4-8**), choose Change Account Picture. The PC Settings screen appears.

Select for fast access to
the PC Settings screen

Figure 4-8

 If you have an e-mail address already, skip to the
section "Use an Existing E-mail Address for a
Microsoft Account."

2. On the left of the PC Settings screen, select the Users
category. Your account information appears with *Local
Account* under your name, as shown in **Figure 4-9**.

Figure 4-9

 If you see *Microsoft Account* instead of *Local Account*,
you already have a Microsoft Account and don't need
to follow these steps.

3. Select the Switch to a Microsoft Account button. Enter your current password (if any) and select Next. The Sign in with a Microsoft Account screen appears. To create a new e-mail address, select Sign Up for a New Email Address (at the bottom of the screen).

4. On the Sign Up for a New Email Address screen (see **Figure 4-10**), in the Email Address box, type the name you want to use (no spaces). Common names have probably been claimed by others and are unavailable. If you type a name that is already taken, you'll get an error message to that effect, but not until several steps later (you can change your choice then). Unusual names, especially full names, may work. Adding some numbers to your name may make it unique, such as *your-firstname-lastname-*12345.

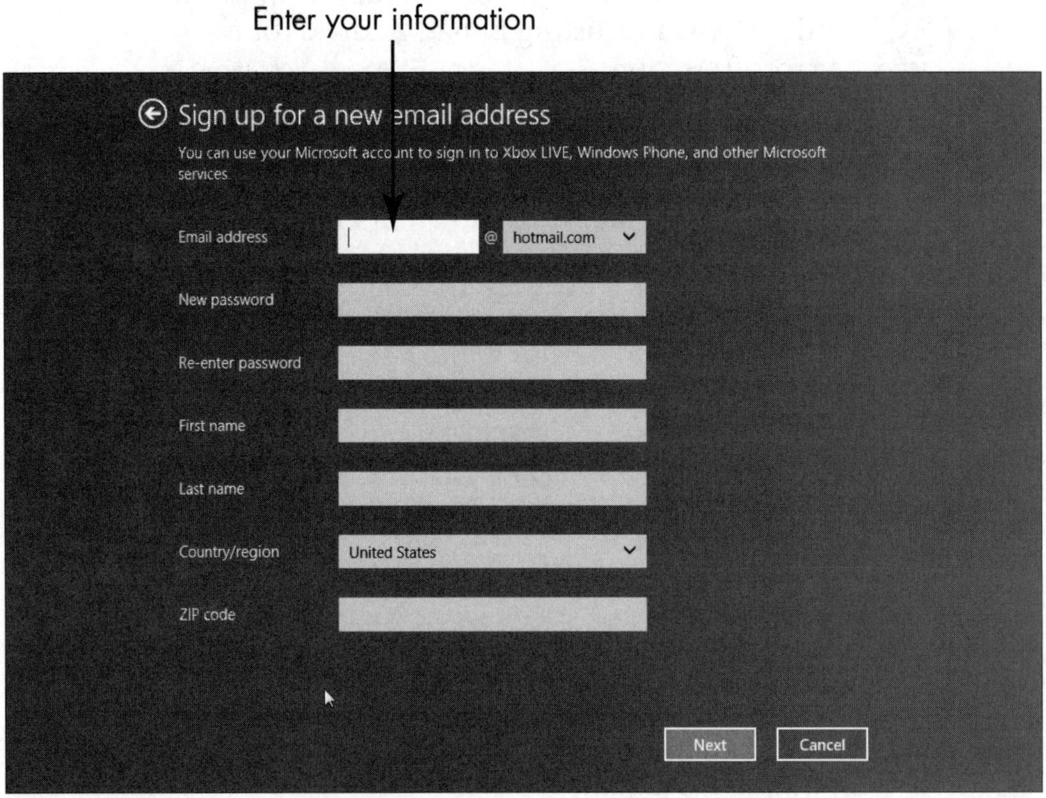

Enter your information

Figure 4-10

5. Next to the @ sign after your name, choose between one of the available services. I know of no specific advantage to one or the other service.

6. In the New Password box, type a password. Dots appear instead of what you type. Use between 7 and 16 characters. Mix uppercase and lowercase, numbers, and symbols such as hyphens (but no spaces).

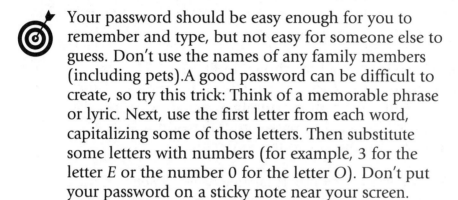 Your password should be easy enough for you to remember and type, but not easy for someone else to guess. Don't use the names of any family members (including pets).A good password can be difficult to create, so try this trick: Think of a memorable phrase or lyric. Next, use the first letter from each word, capitalizing some of those letters. Then substitute some letters with numbers (for example, 3 for the letter *E* or the number 0 for the letter *O*). Don't put your password on a sticky note near your screen.

7. As you move from the Password box, Windows 8 evaluates your password for *strength* (difficulty to guess or deduce). If your password is too simple (such as, *password* or *secret*), the message *Choose a password that's harder for people to guess* appears next to the box. Try a more difficult password.

8. In the Re-Enter Password box, type the same password. If this password doesn't match the one in Step 6, the message *These passwords don't match* appears next to the box.

9. Type your first and last names in the appropriate boxes.

10. If your country or region is not preselected, select your country. Use any of the following methods to move through the list to your country name:

- **Mouse:** Click in the box. Roll the mouse wheel up or down. Click your country name.

- **Touchscreen:** Drag the list up or down. Tap your country name.

- **Keyboard:** Type the first letter of your country or use the arrow keys to move up and down the list. With your country selected, press the Enter or Tab key.

11. Type your ZIP or postal code in the appropriate box. Leave this box blank if it is not applicable to you. Review your entries. Select the Next button, and the Add Security Verification Info screen appears

12. In the Mobile Phone box, shown in **Figure 4-11**, select your country again (using the methods in Step 9). In the next box, enter your phone number, including area code. If you have to reset your password, Microsoft may use this number to confirm your identity.

Although the first box is labeled *Mobile Phone*, the number you enter doesn't have to be a mobile or cell phone number.

13. If you have an alternate e-mail address, you can type it in the Alternate Email box. The alternate e-mail address enables you to receive e-mail from Microsoft if you can't access the account you're setting up.

14. In the box next to Secret Question, select one.

15. In the Answer box, type an answer to the selected question. Hint: The answer doesn't have to be true, just memorable and at least 5 characters. Your answer to the selected question may be used to verify your identity. Because case and punctuation matter, remember your answer exactly as you type it. Then select Next.

16. On the Finish up screen, shown in **Figure 4-12**, select the month, day, and year of your birth. (You can lie, if you remember your response.) Then select your gender.

Enter a phone number

Figure 4-11

17. In the Enter These Characters box, you see some odd characters. These are a test that eliminates non-humans from creating an account (seriously). In the box below those characters, type what you see.

If you can't recognize the characters, select New for a different set of characters or Audio to have the characters read aloud.

18. If you don't want to receive promotional offers and surveys, select the check box to remove the check mark next to Send Me Email.

19. You can select the links to the Microsoft service agreement and privacy statement if you want to read what you're about to agree with. Be the first.

Select New if you can't read the characters in the box

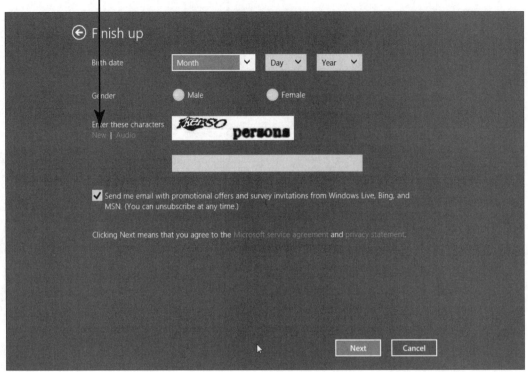

Figure 4-12

20. Select the Next button to finish creating your new Microsoft Account and new e-mail address.

21. You return to the Users category of the PC Settings screen. Note your account name and associated e-mail address (see **Figure 4-13**).

Now you have a Microsoft Account

Figure 4-13

Skip the section "Use an Existing E-Mail Address for a Microsoft Account."

Use an Existing E-Mail Address for a Microsoft Account

1. Follow these steps to switch your Windows 8 user account from local to a Microsoft Account using an existing e-mail address. On the Start screen, select your name in the upper-right corner of the screen, and then choose Change Account Picture from the pop-up menu that appears (refer to **Figure 4-8**).

 If you don't have an e-mail address already, see "Create a New E-Mail Address for a Microsoft Account."

2. On the left side of the PC Settings screen, select the Users category. Your account information appears with *Local Account* under your name (refer to **Figure 4-9**).

 If you see *Microsoft Account* instead of *Local Account* under your user account name, you already have a Microsoft Account and don't need to follow these steps.

3. Select the Switch to a Microsoft Account button. Enter your current password (if any) and select Next. The screen shown in **Figure 4-14** appears. Type the e-mail address you want to associate with your Microsoft Account. Then select the Next button.

4. Microsoft checks the e-mail address you typed to see whether it is already associated with a Microsoft Account. In the unlikely event that you already have a Microsoft Account, type the password for that account, choose Next, confirm the Security verification data, and then choose Next. You return to the Users category of the PC Settings screen (refer to **Figure 4-13**). Note your account name and associated e-mail address. Skip to the next section.

Enter an existing e-mail address

Figure 4-14

5. If the e-mail address you entered in Step 3 is not associ-ated with a Microsoft account, you see the Set Up a Microsoft Account screen, as shown in **Figure** 4-15. The e-mail address you previously typed appears next to the Email Address box. You can change that address here, if appropriate.

6. Follow Steps 6–21 in the preceding section, "Create a New E-Mail Address for a Microsoft Account."

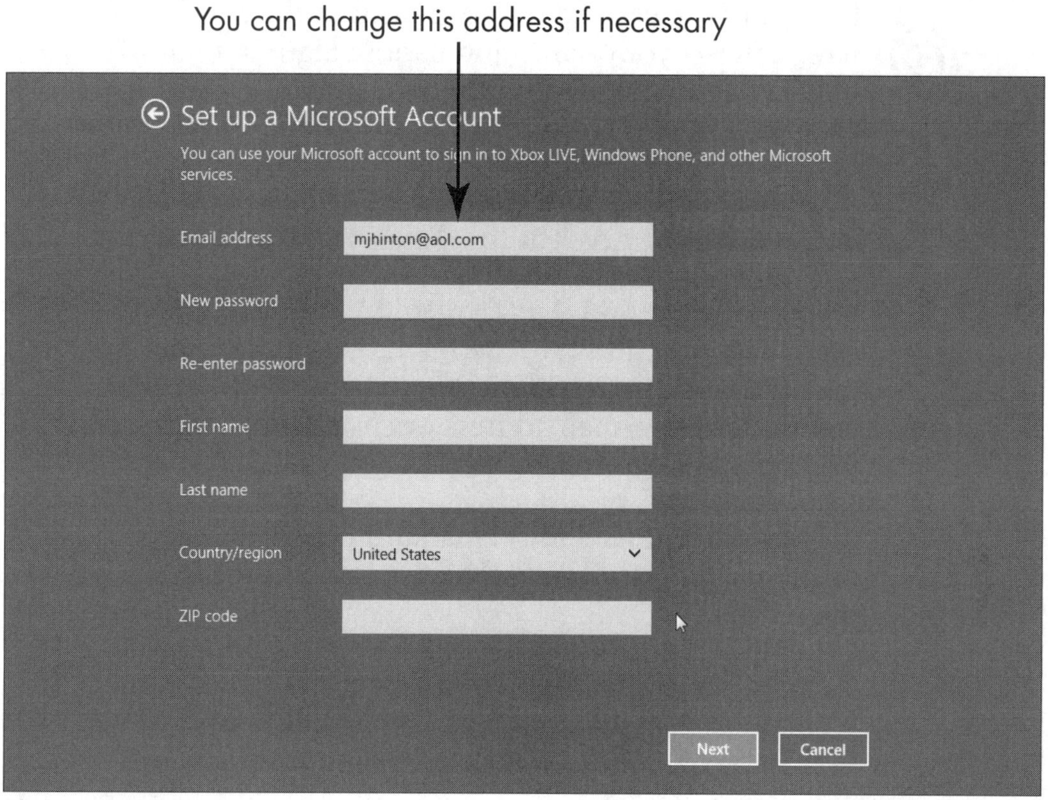

You can change this address if necessary

Figure 4-15

Add a New User

1. You already have the only user account you require on your computer. However, you may want to create an account for someone in your household or as a practice account. Select your name on the Start screen. Choose Change Account Picture from the menu that appears (refer to **Figure 4-8**). The PC Settings screen appears.

2. On the left, select the Users category. On the right, under Other Users, select Add a User. The Add a User screen appears.

If you can't select Add a User, return to the Start screen. Select your name and choose Sign Out. On the Sign In screen, choose the account you created in Chapter 1.

3. At the bottom of the Add a User screen, choose Sign in without a Microsoft Account to create a local account.

 If you know you want a Microsoft Account instead of a local account, jump to Step 3 in one of the two previous sections, depending on whether you want to use an existing e-mail address or create a new one for this new user.

4. On the next screen, read the explanation of your two options for signing in. Then select the Local Account button.

5. On the next screen (see **Figure 4-16**), enter the user name in the first box. Use the person's first name, last name, first and last name, initials, nickname — something easy to remember and type.

Only the user name is required for a local account

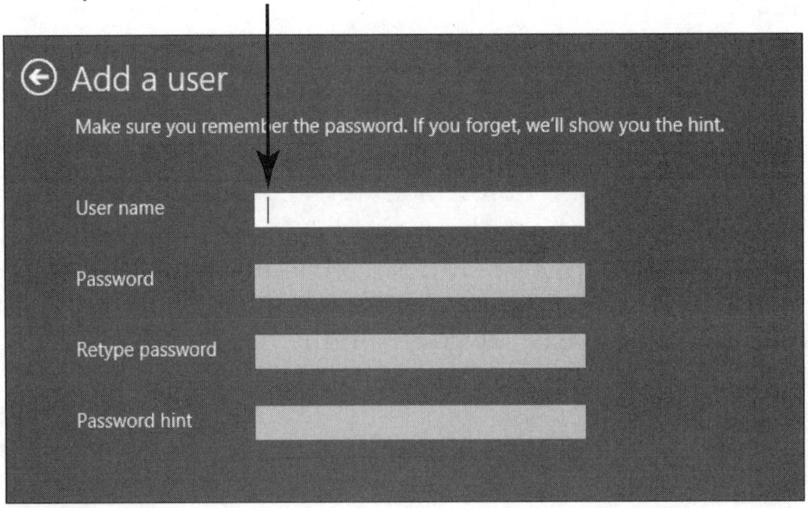

Add a user

Make sure you remember the password. If you forget, we'll show you the hint.

User name

Password

Retype password

Password hint

Figure 4-16

You are not required to use a password with a local account, which makes signing in easy. However, without a password, anyone can use the computer and access information you might want to protect.

6. In the Password box, enter a password. Dots will appear for each character you type.

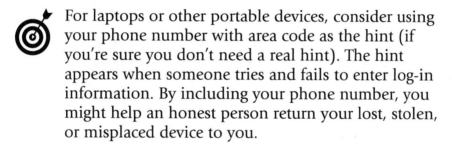 For suggestions on creating a good password, see the tip in Step 6 in the previous section, "Create a New E-Mail Address for a Microsoft Account."

7. In the Retype Password box, type the same password exactly.

8. In the Password Hint box, type a reminder only you will understand.

For laptops or other portable devices, consider using your phone number with area code as the hint (if you're sure you don't need a real hint). The hint appears when someone tries and fails to enter log-in information. By including your phone number, you might help an honest person return your lost, stolen, or misplaced device to you.

9. After completing all the available boxes, choose the Next button. You may see an error message if you left a required field empty, your passwords don't match, or the user name already exists on this computer. If you do see an error, correct your mistake and choose Next again.

10. On the final screen, shown in **Figure 4-17,** you see the new user name next to a generic user picture. Note the option to indicate that this new account belongs to a child. Select this option if you want to receive e-mail reports on the child's computer usage. Select the Finish button. The PC Settings screen appears, with the new user name under Other Users.

The new user name

Figure 4-17

 If family safety options interest you, type **family** on the Start screen, select Settings on the right, and then select Family Safety on the left. The Family Safety function opens on the desktop. See the website www.win8mjh.com for more information.

11. Return to the Start screen. In the upper-right corner of the screen, select your user name. In the drop-down menu that appears, select the new user name to switch to that account.

12. A screen appears with the new user name. If you used a password on the new user account, type that password in the box and select the on-screen right arrow or press Enter.

 The first time you sign in as a new user, an animation demonstrates that you can move your mouse to any corner or, if you have a touchscreen, swipe from any edge. The color of the screen and the text on-screen changes a few times to keep you mesmerized as setup finishes. Your new account will be ready in just a moment. Then the generic Start screen appears. (Any settings you changed in your account do not transfer to other accounts.)

13. In the upper-right corner of the Start screen, choose the new user name. Note that the old user name is labeled *Signed In*, as shown in **Figure 4-18**. Both accounts are signed in. You can switch between them by selecting the user name you want to switch to. To sign out of an account, choose Sign Out.

All users are listed here

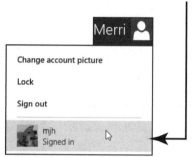

Figure 4-18

 For information on personalizing the Lock and Start screens for the new account, see Chapter 3.

Create a Password

1. On the Start screen, select your name. From the drop-down menu that appears, choose Change Account Picture (refer to **Figure 4-8**). The PC Settings screen appears.

 If you already have a password, see the section "Change or Remove Your Password."

2. On the left, select the Users category (refer to **Figure 4-9**).

3. If you don't have a password but want one, select the Create a Password button under Sign-In Options.

 The buttons available under Sign-in Options depend on your current setup. You may see buttons that enable you to create, change, or remove a particular setting.

4. In the Create a Password screen, shown in **Figure** 4-19, enter a password in the New Password box.

Figure 4-19

 For a local account, the password can be any length. See Step 6 in the previous section, "Create a New E-Mail Address for a Microsoft Account," for suggestions about creating a good password

5. In the Retype Password box, enter the password again.

6. Enter a hint to remind yourself — and no one else — about your password.

7. Select Next. If any error messages appear, correct the entries and select Next again.

8. The final Create a Password screen indicates you must use your new password the next time you sign in. Select Finish.

Change or Remove Your Password

1. On the Start screen, select your name, and then choose Change Account Picture. On the left side of the PC Settings screen, select Users.

2. If you want to change your password, select the Change Your Password button Under Sign-In Options.

If you don't have a password but want one, see the section "Create a Password."

3. On the Change Your Password screen, enter your current password and then select the Next button.

4. On the next Change Your Password screen (see **Figure 4-20**), enter the new password.

 To remove your current password and use no password, leave all boxes blank.

 For a local account, the password can be any length. Microsoft Account passwords must be between 7 and 16 characters and sufficiently complex, as determined by Windows 8.

If you don't want a password, leave these boxes blank

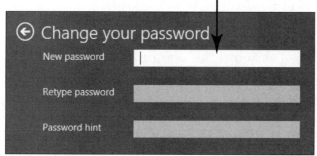

Figure 4-20

5. In the Retype Password box, enter the password again.

6. Enter a hint to remind yourself — and no one else — about your password. Then select Next. If any error messages appear, correct the entries and select Next again.

7. The final screen indicates you must use your new password the next time you sign in. (This message appears even if you left the password blank, in which case you won't need any password.) Select Finish.

Create a Picture Password

1. Intended for a touchscreen, a *picture password* uses a photo you select. During setup, you draw three gestures on the photo. You then sign in to your computer by drawing the same three gestures in the same areas of the picture. Some consider this method easier than entering a traditional password. On the Start screen, select your name and then choose Change Account Picture from the drop-down menu.

2. On the left side of the PC Settings screen, select Users.

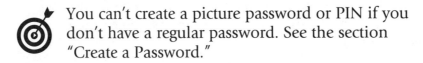 You can't create a picture password or PIN if you don't have a regular password. See the section "Create a Password."

3. If you don't have a Picture Password but want one, select the Create a Picture Password button under Sign-In Options.

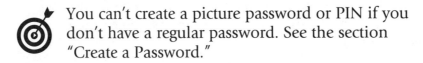 If you have a Picture Password but want to change or remove it, see the next section, "Change or Remove Your Picture Password."

4. On the next screen, enter your current password. Select the OK button.

5. Read the text on the Welcome to Picture Password screen. Note that the size, position, and direction of your gestures become part of your picture password. Select the Choose Picture button.

6. On the next screen, shown in **Figure 4-21**, select the photo you want to use and then select the Open button.

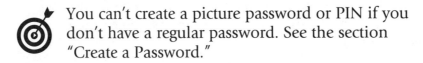 See Chapter 10 for information on using your own photos.

Select a photo, then select Open

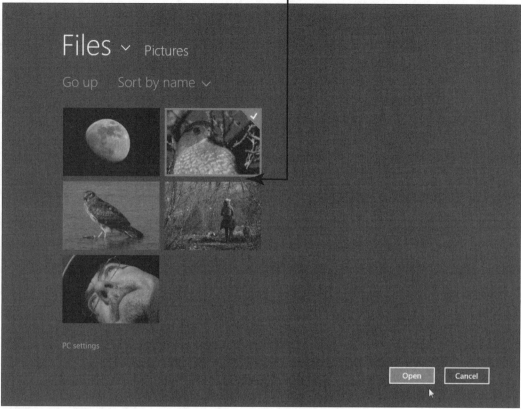

Figure 4-21

7. On the How's This Look? screen, drag the photo if you need to position it differently. Then select the Use This Picture button. (If you want to use another picture, select the Choose New Picture button and repeat Step 6. A check mark indicates the currently selected photo.)

8. On the Set Up Your Gestures screen, shown in **Figure 4-22**), draw three gestures on the photo. Draw circles, straight lines, or simply tap areas. As you draw or tap, the screen shows briefly the gestures you make.

Draw on the photo using circles, lines, or taps

Figure 4-22

9. The Confirm Your Gestures screen appears automatically after you draw the third gesture in Step 8. Repeat the gestures, using the same position, size, and direction. If your gestures don't match those in Step 8, the Something's Not Right screen appears. Choose between Try Again, Start Over or Cancel.

10. When you have successfully repeated the gestures, you see a Congratulations screen. Select Finish. The next time you sign in, your password photo will appear. Make the same three gestures you made in Step 8 to sign into Windows 8. No password required.

On the sign-in screen, you have an option to switch to a password screen, even if you have set up a picture password. This feature enables you to sign in with your password if you can't repeat the required gestures.

Change or Remove Your Picture Password

1. On the Start screen, select your name and then choose Change Account Picture. On the PC Settings screen, select Users.

2. If you don't want to use a picture password, select the Remove button under Sign-In Options. One click and your picture password is gone without further confirmation. Skip the remaining steps.

3. If you want to change your picture password, select the Change Picture Password button under Sign-In Options.

4. On the screen that displays *First, confirm your current password*, enter your password. Then, select OK.

5. On the Change Your Picture Password screen (shown in **Figure 4-23**), select one of the following options:

- **Use This Picture:** Select this option if you want to use the same picture with new gestures. On the next screen, draw three gestures on the photo, and then repeat those gestures on the next screen, which appears automatically. See Steps 8–10 in the section "Create a Picture Password."

- **Choose New Picture:** Use this option to both select a different photo and create new gestures. See Steps 6–10 in the section "Create a Picture Password."

- **Replay:** Select this option if you need to see the gestures you used for the picture password. After the gestures are replayed, you reenter the gestures twice.

Figure 4-23

Create a PIN

1. A *PIN* (personal identification number) has two advantages over a password. One, a PIN consists of just four numbers, so it's easier to remember and enter, especially with a virtual keyboard. Two, you don't press the Enter key with a PIN, making it even faster to use. (I use a PIN on my home computer.) On the Start screen, select your user name and then choose Change Account Picture.

2. On the PC Settings screen, select Users. Under Sign-In Options, select the Create a PIN button.

 If you have a PIN but want to change or remove it, see the section "Change or Remove Your Pin."

You can't create a picture password or PIN if you don't have a regular password. See the section "Create a Password."

3. On the next screen, enter your current password and then select OK.

4. On the Create a PIN screen, shown in **Figure** 4-24, enter four digits in the first box. Re-enter those four digits in the second box. Select Finish. The next time you sign in, enter your four-digit pin.

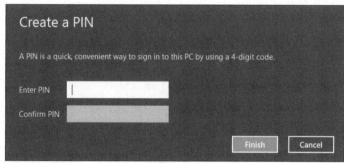

Create a PIN

A PIN is a quick, convenient way to sign in to this PC by using a 4-digit code.

Enter PIN

Confirm PIN

Finish   Cancel

Figure 4-24

 On the sign-in screen, you can switch to a password screen, even if you have a PIN. This feature enables you to sign in if you don't remember your PIN.

Change or Remove Your PIN

1. Select your name on the Start screen, and then choose Change account picture. On the PC Settings screen, select the Users category on the left

2. If you don't want to use a PIN, select the Remove button under Sign-In Options. One click and the PIN is gone without further confirmation. Skip the remaining steps.

 If you don't have a PIN but want one, see the section "Create a PIN."

3. If you want to change your PIN, select the Change PIN button under Sign-In Options. On the verification screen, enter your current password and select OK.

4. On the Change Your PIN screen, enter a new four-digit PIN in the first box.

5. In the Confirm New PIN box, reenter your new PIN. (A message appears if the PINs don't match.) Select Finish. The next time you sign in, enter your new four-digit pin.

Delete a User Account

1. Before you delete a user account, make sure that account is signed out. Then sign in to the administrator account, which is the one you created in Chapter 1.

2. On the Start menu, type *remove user* to search for matching functions. Select the Settings category on the right side of the Search screen. On the left, select Remove User Accounts (see **Figure 4-25**). The desktop appears on your screen. Certain functions, particularly more advanced or less common functions such as deleting a user account, run on the desktop. See Chapter 5 for information on using the desktop.

3. In the Manage Accounts window, shown in **Figure 4-26**, select the account you want to delete. The Change an Account window appears. On the left, select Delete the Account.

3. Select this　　　　　　　　　　　　　　　　1. Type this

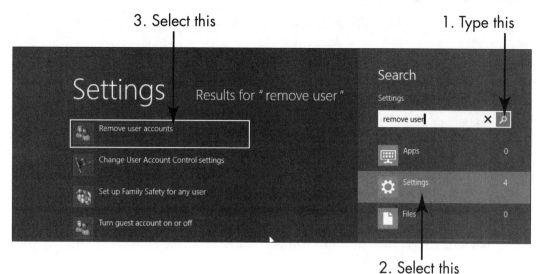

Figure 4-25

2. Select this

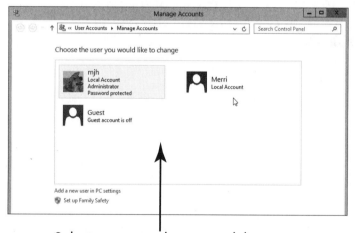

Select a user to change or delete

Figure 4-26

 To go back to the previous window, select the arrow in a circle in the upper-left corner of the screen.

4. In the Delete Account window, you decide what to do with local documents and photos in the account you are deleting. Choose one of the following buttons:

- **Delete Files:** Erases all files belonging to the user.

- **Keep Files:** Copies files from the desktop and other user folders into a new folder on the administrator's desktop. The folder will have the name of the deleted user.

- **Cancel:** Does nothing.

 If you're not sure which option is best, choose Keep Files or Cancel.

5. On the Confirm Deletion screen, select the Delete Account button.

6. You're done with the desktop for now. Return to the Start screen by clicking in the lower-left corner of the screen, by swiping from the right edge to the left and tapping Start, or by pressing ⊞.

Getting Comfortable with the Desktop

*I*n Windows 8, the *desktop* is an app you
access through a tile on the Start screen.
Unlike other apps, the desktop is an environ-
ment for using programs that pre-date the new
Windows 8 apps. The desktop enables
Windows 8 users to run older programs.
Microsoft takes pains not to break abruptly
with the past as it paves the way for the future.

You may find yourself on the desktop as a
result of choosing an app from the Start screen,
Search Results screen, or All Apps screen. For
that reason alone, take the time to explore the
desktop-way of doing things, which is not
quite the new Windows 8 way.

One key feature of the desktop is the *taskbar*, a
strip along the bottom of the screen that shows
icons for desktop programs. The taskbar can be
used to run and switch between desktop programs. Most programs on the desktop run in
windows, as opposed to the full-screen nature
of Windows 8 apps.

In this chapter, you get acquainted with the desktop, the taskbar, and windowed apps. You change the date, time, and time zone, as needed. You resize and reposition windowed apps. You select a background for the desktop and make some desktop apps more convenient to use by pinning them to the taskbar. Finally, you work with the Task Manager, which lets you end any app — desktop or Windows 8.

 The desktop originated when using the mouse was the most common method for selecting objects (touchscreens were nonexistent). Therefore, on the desktop, a few tasks are easier to do with the mouse than with touch or keyboard.

 This chapter is an introduction to the desktop. See Part IV to dive a little deeper into desktop functions, such as organizing documents.

Check Out the Desktop

1. On the Start screen, select the Desktop tile to display the desktop. Your desktop will have a picture in the background.

 Most people like to display a photo on their desktop. For details, see the section "Choose a Desktop Background."

 Some computers don't have the Desktop tile.

2. Examine your desktop for *icons* — small pictures that represent either programs, which perform functions, or documents, such as letters and photos. You select an icon to run a program or open a document. The Windows 8 desktop displays an icon for the Recycle Bin, where deleted documents go. The Recycle Bin may be the only icon on your desktop, or you may see others. See Chapter 14 for information on using the Recycle Bin.

3. The area at the bottom of the screen is the *taskbar*, where you see icons for some programs as shown in **Figure 5-1**. The first two icons, for example, are for programs that are available but not currently running (Microsoft Internet Explorer and File Explorer, respectively).

Taskbar　　　　　　　　　Virtual keyboard

Icon tray

Figure 5-1

 You can use the taskbar to switch between programs by selecting the icon for the program you want to use.

4. The right end of the taskbar is an area called the *icon tray*, which displays the current date and time, as well as icons for other programs that run automatically when your computer starts. Select an icon in the icon tray to open the associated program.

 You select items on the desktop or in the taskbar by clicking with the mouse or tapping the touchscreen. To some extent, you can use the Tab and arrow keys, but that's an awkward method.

 If you have a touchscreen, note the taskbar icon for the virtual keyboard (refer to **Figure 5-1**). See Chapter 1 for information about using the keyboard.

5. Right-click over an icon or tap and hold until a small box appears, then release. A *context menu* appears with options specific to the icon you selected. Select anywhere else on the desktop to dismiss this menu. Repeat this on a few different areas of the screen to see how the context menu changes.

If you can select the item using the keyboard, you can then press the context menu key to display the menu.

Change the Date or Time

1. Select the date and time displayed in the taskbar. A calendar and clock pop up, as shown in **Figure** 5-2.

Figure 5-2

2. If the date or time is incorrect, select Change Date and Time Settings. In the Date and Time window that appears, select the Change Date and Time button.

3. In the Date and Time Settings window, shown in **Figure 5-3**, select the correct date in the calendar. Then change the time by using the little triangles that point up (later) or down (earlier) or by entering the specific hours and minutes. Select OK to keep your change or Cancel to ignore your change.

4. Back in the Date and Time window, select Change Time Zone.

5. In the Time Zone Settings window, shown in **Figure 5-4**, select the Time Zone drop-down menu and then select your time zone. Select (add a check mark) or deselect the Daylight Saving Time option as appropriate. Select OK to keep your change or Cancel to ignore your change.

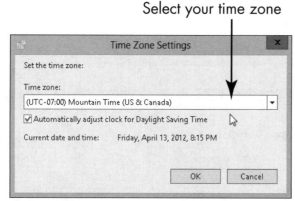

Figure 5-3

Figure 5-4

You can also check or change the time zone or Daylight Saving Time setting using PC Settings⇨General⇨Time.

Explore the Parts of a Window

1. In the taskbar, select the second icon from the left, which looks like a folder. File Explorer opens, as shown in **Figure 5-5**.

Quick Access toolbar

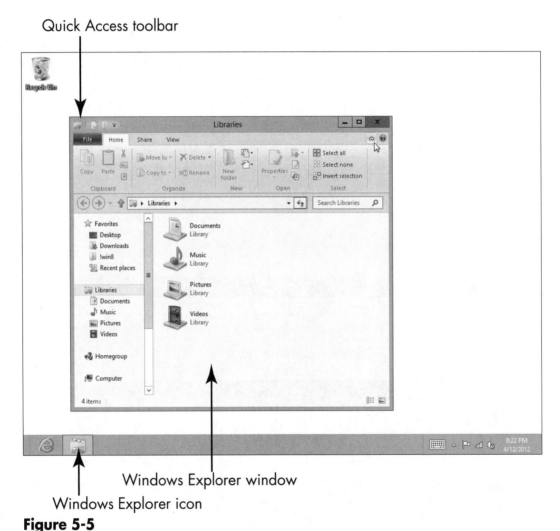

Windows Explorer window

Windows Explorer icon

Figure 5-5

File Explorer enables you to view your computer storage, such as hard disks, and folders, which are used to organize your documents. See Chapter 14 for information on using File Explorer.

 File Explorer is not the same as Microsoft Internet Explorer, the web browser (and the first icon in the taskbar). See Chapter 6 for information on using Microsoft Internet Explorer to browse the Web.

2. Explore the example window in **Figure 5-5,** starting at the top left:

- **Quick Access toolbar:** The *Quick Access toolbar* gives you fast access to common operations, such as saving a document. This toolbar is not present in all windows and may feature different functions, depending on the window.

- **Title bar:** The *title bar,* which is the top line of the window, contains the title of the desktop program you're using. When you use a program to create a document, the name of the document also appears in the title bar.

 The title of the window in **Figure 5-5** is Libraries, the location File Explorer is focused on when you open File Explorer. Libraries contain all your files.

- *Minimize:* The *Minimize button* shrinks or hides the window's contents. The program that the window contains is still running and open, but the window is out of sight. You'll still see the program's icon in the taskbar. Select the Minimize button when you want to ignore a particular window but aren't actually done with it. To restore the window, select its icon in the taskbar.

- *Maximize/Restore:* The *Maximize button* (the button with a single square) fills the screen with the contents of the window. Select the Maximize button to hide the desktop and other open windows, to concentrate on one window, and to see as much of the window's contents as you can. The *Restore button* (the button with two squares) is the name of the button that appears after you select the Maximize button; it replaces the Maximize button. Select the Restore button to return the window to its previous size, which is between maximized and minimized. (Press ⊞+up arrow key to maximize, and ⊞+down arrow key to restore or minimize.)

- *Close: The Close button* is the red button with the X in the top-right corner of the window. Select the Close button when you are done with the window. Close is also called Quit and Exit. (Press Alt+F4 to close the current window or the desktop itself. This keyboard shortcut works for Windows 8 apps, as well.)

- **Ribbon:** The *ribbon* is a toolbar that provides access to many functions organized as groups within tabs. The tabs appear across the top of the ribbon. The first time you run File Explorer, the ribbon is hidden (collapsed). Display the ribbon by selecting the caret symbol (^) on the far right, next to Help (the question mark). Select the caret again to hide the ribbon. You can also press Ctrl+F1 to toggle the ribbon on and off. (Leave the ribbon visible for this chapter.) The tabs remain in view and function the same. Although ribbons vary between programs, most ribbons have File, Home, and View tabs. In **Figure 5-5**, File Explorer has a Share tab, as well. To use a tab, select its name to display its functions, and then select the item you want to use.

The ribbon can help you discover new functions.

- **Contents:** The bulk of the window contains the program or document you're using. File Explorer displays locations on the left and objects in that location on the right.

- **Status bar:** Along the bottom edge of the window, some programs display information about the window or its contents in a single-line *status bar*. File Explorer does not have a status bar.

Scan the edges of windows. Often, important information and functions are pushed to these edges around the main content area.

3. Select the Close button (the red X) to close File Explorer.

Although the Quick Access toolbar and the Close button work on a touchscreen, they are small targets. You may find a stylus more accurate when dealing with smaller elements.

See Chapter 2 for information on finding other desktop programs, such as the Calculator.

Resize a Window

1. To resize a window, open File Explorer by selecting the folder icon in the taskbar. (Refer to **Figure 5-5**.)

 2. If the window is maximized (fills the screen), select the Restore button to make the window smaller.

3. Use one of these methods to resize the window:

- **Mouse:** Move the mouse pointer to the right edge of the window, until the pointer changes to a double-headed arrow called the *resize pointer*. Click and drag the edge of the window, using the resize pointer. (To drag, click and hold down the mouse button while you move the mouse.)

- **Touchscreen:** Drag the right edge of the window.

 Drag left to shrink the window and right to expand it.

4. Resize the window's width and height at the same time by dragging a corner of the window (see **Figure 5-6**). If you want a challenge, try resizing the top-right corner without accidentally selecting the Close button.

5. Resize the window's width *or* height by dragging any of the four sides.

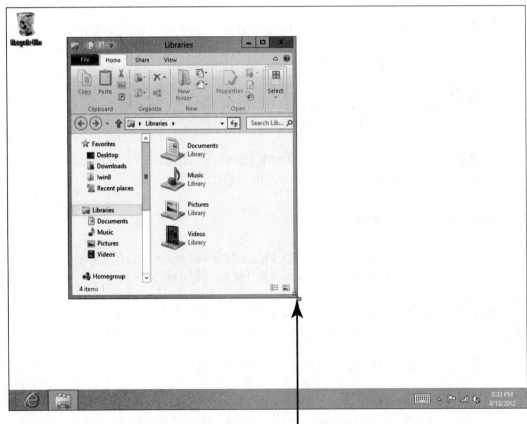

Drag the corner with the mouse or your finger to resize the window

Figure 5-6

You may want to resize a window to show only what you need to see, nothing more. Practice resizing from any side or corner.

6. Leave the window open as you go on to the next task.

Arrange Some Windows

1. On the desktop, select and open the Recycle Bin by double-clicking or double-tapping its icon. The Recycle Bin contains deleted files and folders. It appears in another File Explorer window. See **Figure 5-7**.

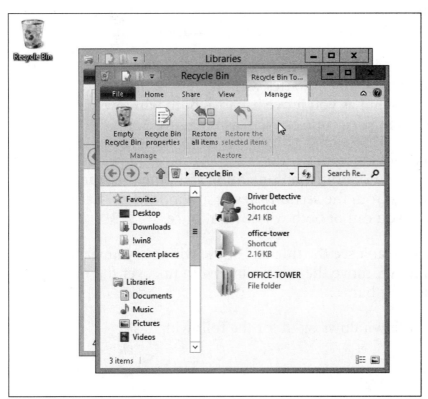

Figure 5-7

 Double-click by clicking the left mouse button twice, without a pause. Double-tap by tapping twice in quick succession.

2. If File Explorer isn't still open from the preceding section, open it by selecting the folder icon in the taskbar. You now see two overlapping windows on the desktop (refer to **Figure 5-7**), one titled *Libraries* and the other titled *Recycle Bin*.

 The window in front of the others is called the *active* window. All other windows are *inactive*. Note that the title bar of the active window is a different color from the title bar in any inactive window. Selecting anywhere in an inactive window makes it active and moves it to the front of the others.

3. Drag the Recycle Bin title bar (avoiding the buttons on the left and right ends) to move that window a little.

4. Drag the Libraries title bar (again, avoiding the buttons on both ends). The Libraries window moves in front of the Recycle Bin as you move it. Move both windows so that you can see a little of each, as in **Figure 5-8**.

5. Practice moving both windows. Arranging windows helps you see and do more than one thing at a time. Use the techniques from the section "Resize a Window" to see as much as you can of both windows at once.

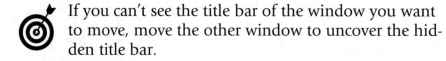 If you can't see the title bar of the window you want to move, move the other window to uncover the hidden title bar.

6. Leave both windows open for the following task.

Move a window by dragging its title bar

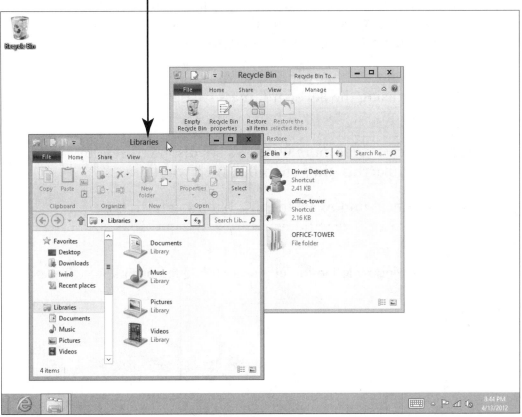

Figure 5-8

Snap a Window

1. Drag one of the windows you worked with in the preceding section to the left edge of the screen. When the mouse pointer or your finger touches the left edge of the screen, you'll see an outline on the screen, as shown in

Figure 5-9. Release the window, and it resizes automatically to fill the left half of the screen, as shown in **Figure 5-10**. This procedure is called *snap*. (To snap a window using the keyboard, press ⊞+left arrow.)

2. Now snap the other window to the right. (To move the window using the keyboard, press ⊞+right arrow.) It resizes and fills the right half of the screen.

> When two or more windows are displayed side by side like this, they are called **tiled** windows.

3. Drag either window by the title bar away from the edge of the screen. The window returns to its previous size.

Drag the window to the far left   Note the outline

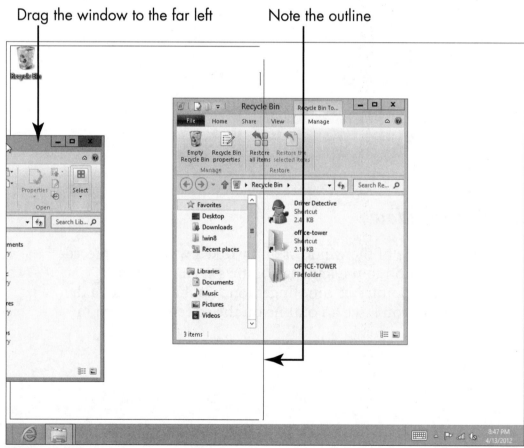

Figure 5-9

Release the window to complete the snap

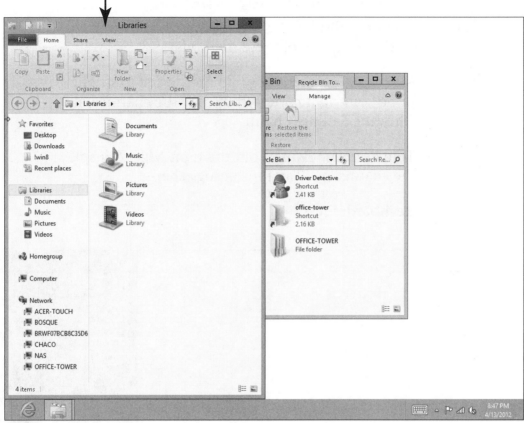

Figure 5-10

4. Drag either window to the top edge of the screen. This action maximizes the window, just as though you selected the Maximize button (see the section "Explore the Parts of a Window").

5. Drag the title bar of the maximized window away from the top to restore it to its previous size, just as though you selected the Restore button.

6. Close or minimize both windows.

Choose a Desktop Background

1. On the desktop, display the Settings panel, shown in **Figure** 5-11, using one of these methods:

- **Mouse:** Move the mouse pointer to the top-right or bottom-right corner to display the charms bar. Click the Settings charm.

- **Touchscreen:** Swipe from the right edge to display the charms bar. Tap the Settings charm.

- **Keyboard:** Press ⊞+I.

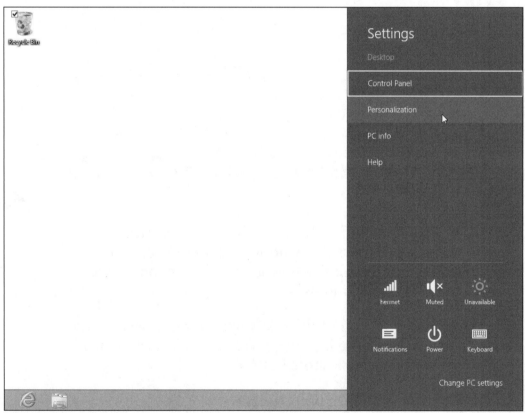

Figure 5-11

2. Select Personalization. The Personalization window opens, as shown in **Figure 5-12**.

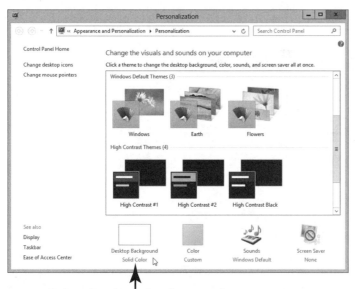

Select Desktop Background

Figure 5-12

 You can use the Personalization window to customize many aspects of the desktop. The more time you spend on the desktop and not on the Start screen, the more worthwhile this personalization may be.

3. In the Personalization window, select the Desktop Background option (at the bottom). The Desktop Background window appears, as shown in **Figure 5-13**.

4. Select any photo to make that photo the desktop background. The background changes immediately. To see the entire desktop, minimize the current window. Restore the Desktop Background window by selecting its icon in the taskbar or by repeating the preceding steps.

 The background you choose here will also appear on the Desktop tile on the Start screen. That's pretty cool.

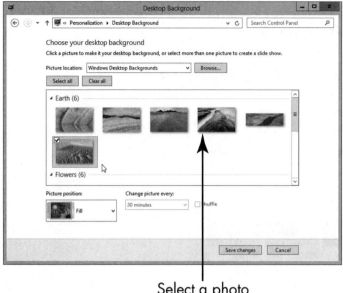

Select a photo

Figure 5-13

5. Select more than one photo for the background as
   follows:

   • Select individual photos using the check box in the
     upper-left corner of each thumbnail. Select again
     to remove that check mark.

   • Select all photos under a heading, such as Earth,
     by selecting the heading.

   • Use the Select All button to select all photos.
     (Yeah, that was obvious.) Select the Clear All but-
     ton to unselect all photos.

6. Select the Change Picture Every option to change the
   amount of time that passes before the next picture is displayed. Intervals range from every 10 seconds to once per
   day. For a quick test of this feature, choose 10 seconds.

7. If you want to mix the order in which the photos appear, select the Shuffle check box.

8. Minimize the Desktop Background window. The desktop background changes every 10 seconds (unless you chose a different frequency or chose only one photo). Restore the Desktop Background window by selecting its icon on the taskbar.

You can find pictures also in the Pictures Library, Top Rated Photos (based on ratings you give to your own photos), and Solid Colors (such as white). See Chapter 10 for information on adding photos to the Pictures Library.

9. To keep the selections you make in the Desktop Background window, select the Save Changes button (refer to **Figure 5-13**). To undo those selections, select Cancel. In either case, you return to the Personalization window. Close the Personalization window when you are done with it.

Pin Icons to the Taskbar

1. On the Start screen, type *calculator* to search for that desktop program. Then select the Calculator tile and display the app bar, shown in **Figure 5-14**, using one of these methods:

- **Mouse:** Right-click the Calculator tile.

- **Touchscreen:** Swipe the Calculator tile down or up slightly.

- **Keyboard:** Press the Tab key to highlight the Calculator tile. Press the context menu key, usually found to the right of the spacebar.

Select the tile

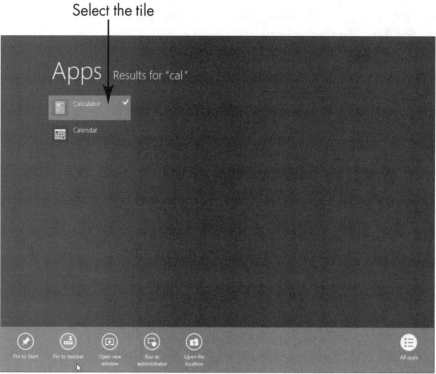

Figure 5-14

2. Select the Pin to Taskbar button. Doing so places the icon for Calculator in the desktop taskbar for easy access.

3. Switch to the Start screen. Then display the desktop by selecting the Desktop tile on the Start screen.

Keyboard: Press ⊞+D to go directly to the desktop.

4. The Calculator icon appears in the taskbar, as shown in **Figure 5-15**.

Calculator is pinned

Figure 5-15

5. Return to the Start screen. Repeat Step 1 and then select Unpin from Taskbar.

6. Switch to the desktop. The Calculator icon is gone.

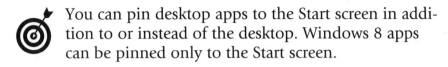 You can pin desktop apps to the Start screen in addition to or instead of the desktop. Windows 8 apps can be pinned only to the Start screen.

Pinned icons have a killer feature: *jumplists*, which are short menus of tasks and documents specific to the pinned app. To see the jumplist of a pinned app, right-click its icon in the taskbar or tap and hold on the icon until a small box appears. Try that with the File Explorer icon in the taskbar. Not all desktop apps have jumplists.

Stop Apps with the Task Manager

1. On the desktop, select Task Manager from the taskbar context menu (shown in **Figure 5-16**) using one of these methods:

- **Mouse:** Right-click over an empty area of the taskbar and select Task Manager from the context menu.

- **Touchscreen:** Tap and hold an empty area of the taskbar until a small box appears, then release. Select Task Manager from the context menu.

- **Keyboard:** Press Ctrl+Shift+Esc to display the Task Manager directly.

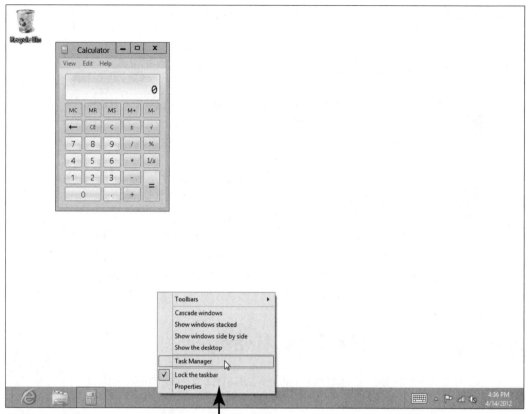

Taskbar context menu

Figure 5-16

 You can search for Task Manager from the Start screen. Then, you could pin it to Start or the taskbar.

2. The Task Manager lists any running apps — both desktop apps, such as Calculator, and Windows 8 apps, such as Weather. Select an app, also referred to as a *task*. Note that the End Task button is now available, as shown in **Figure 5-17**. You don't have to end this task, but you could. Any of the tasks in the Task Manager window can be ended without consequences.

Be careful about ending an app used to create something (for example, a word-processing app) because you could lose data you haven't saved before ending the task. Use the Task Manager to end tasks that you can't end otherwise, such as a frozen or locked app or one that seems to slow down everything.

Select a task

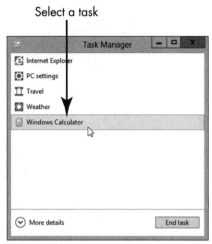

Figure 5-17

3. Select the More Details option. The Task Manager expands and displays detailed information about every process running on the computer. There's more to Task Manager, although you may not need all of its capabilities. Select Fewer Details to return to the simpler version.

4. Close the Task Manager, and then return to the Start screen.

Part II
Windows 8 and the Web

The 5th Wave   By Rich Tennant

"Since we got it, he hasn't moved from that spot for eleven straight days. Oddly enough they call this 'getting up and running' on the Internet."

Finding What You Need on the Web

*T*he World Wide Web — or, simply, the Web — provides quick access to information and entertainment worldwide. One part library, one part marketplace, and one part soapbox, the Web makes everything equidistant: From down the block to halfway around the world — even out into space — everything is a few clicks or taps away. News, shopping, and the electronic equivalent of the town square await you.

You explore the Web using a *web browser*, a program designed to make browsing the Web easy, enjoyable, and safe. In this chapter, I show how you can use Microsoft Internet Explorer to step beyond your computer into the global village.

You browse *web pages*, which are published by governments, businesses, and individuals — anyone can create web pages. Each web page may consist of a few words or thousands of words and pictures. A web page is part of a larger collection called a *website*, which consists of a group of related web pages published on a topic by an organization or individual. Companies and individuals create websites to organize their related pages.

Pages and sites on the Web have some common characteristics:

➡ **Unique addresses,** which are formally called *URLs* (URL stands for Uniform Resource Locator, in case you're ever on *Jeopardy!*).

➡ **Connecting links** that move you from page to page when you select them. These *links* (also called *hypertext links* or *hyperlinks*) often appear underlined and blue. Pictures and other graphic images can also be links to other pages. Exploring the Web using links is easier than typing URLs.

In this chapter, you use Microsoft Internet Explorer to browse the Web. To get the most out of browsing, you juggle multiple sites at once. You find out how to search for almost anything, and you also use the Reader app for certain types of documents frequently found on the Web.

Browse the Web with Microsoft Internet Explorer

1. Open Internet Explorer by selecting its tile on the Start screen. Note the *command bar* at the bottom of the screen in **Figure 6-1**. The address for the current page, if any, appears in the command bar, located at the bottom of the screen. In **Figure 6-1**, the address is www.bing.com. Your screen may look different.

 Each time you open Internet Explorer, you see the default page, called the *home page*, or the page you were browsing last. You may see an error message if you're not connected to the Internet. If so, see Chapter 4 for information on connecting.

2. Select the address box in the command bar. A panel slides up to display tiles under *Frequent* and *Pinned*. You may not see anything under the headings until you browse some sites.

Command bar   Address box

Figure 6-1

 The tiles under *Frequent* and *Pinned* make it easy to return to web pages by simply selecting the tile you want. These tiles become more useful as you continue to browse. Eventually, you have to scroll to the right to see those that don't fit on the first screen.

3. In the address box, type www.win8mjh.com and select the go arrow (right-pointing arrow) or press Enter. The web page for this book appears, as shown in **Figure 6-2**.

 If you don't have a keyboard, see Chapter 1 for information on using the virtual keyboard.

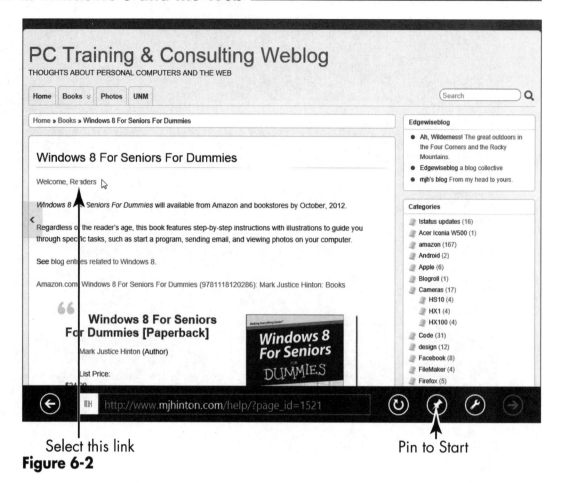

Select this link

Pin to Start

Figure 6-2

 On the book's web page, I post updates and links to recommended resources.

4. Select the Welcome, Readers link with a click or a tap.

 To use the keyboard to select a link, press the Tab key until the link is selected, and then press Enter. (Seeing when the link is selected can be difficult.) I include other keystrokes as you need them.

5. Read the text on the Welcome page. Select the back arrow in the command bar (or press Alt+left arrow) to return to the preceding page. If you see a back arrow on the left side of the screen, you can select that instead.

6. Select the forward arrow (or press Alt+right arrow) to
return to the Welcome page. If you see a forward arrow
on the right side of the screen, you can use that instead.
The browser remembers the pages you visit to make it
easy to go forward and back.

7. Select the address box. The Frequent and Favorites screen
appears, as shown in **Figure 6-3.** Select the Windows 8
for Seniors tile. If you don't see that tile, type **win8mjh**
and select the matching tile or press Enter.

 Browsing the Web consists of entering address, following links, going forward and back, and using the
Frequent tiles. Relatively simple activities that can
absorb hours.

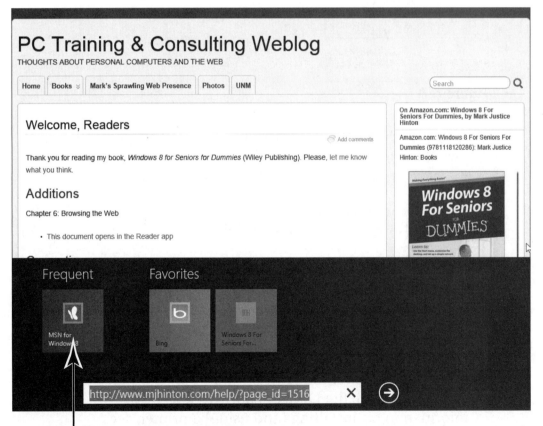

Frequently browsed and pinned pages

Figure 6-3

8. Browse the first book page again. (Use the forward or back arrow or the Frequent tile, or enter www.win8mjh. com.) Select the pushpin button to the right of the address (refer to **Figure 6-2**). The box shown in **Figure 6-4** appears. Select the Pin to Start button.

 You can change the text in the box before you select Pin to Start. However, there's usually no need to change the text unless it's overly long or unclear.

Figure 6-4

9. Return to the Start screen. Scroll to the right to locate the new tile for the book's web page. Select that tile to open the page in Internet Explorer (IE).

10. Select the address box. Note the tile for the book's web page is also under the Pinned heading.

 Pin the pages you want to visit easily. See Chapter 3 for information on unpinning and rearranging the tiles on the Start screen.

11. To print this web page, display the charms bar and then select the Devices charm. In the Devices panel, select a printer. Then, select the Print button to print or select anything outside the Devices panel to cancel. For information on installing (and using) a printer, see Chapter 13.

Some web pages are quite long, requiring more than one page of paper. Be certain you want to print.

12. Return to the Start screen.

 You may encounter web pages that don't open properly in the Windows 8 version of IE because it doesn't support every function found on web pages. See the section "Use Internet Explorer on the Desktop" for information on an alternative for viewing web pages.

Open Multiple Pages in Separate Tabs

1. Select the Internet Explorer tile on the Start screen.

2. Browse the book's website, at www.win8mjh.com.

3. Display the command bar in **Figure 6-5** using one of these methods:

- **Mouse:** Click the right mouse button, making sure the pointer is not over a link, photo, or video.

- **Touchscreen:** Drag down from the top edge or up from the bottom edge.

- **Keyboard:** Press ⊞+Z.

 Use one of these methods if the command bar along the bottom disappears, as it will while you browse a page.

 Is that the *app bar* on top and the *command bar* on the bottom? To my mind, the app bar appears when you use one of the methods in the preceding step. But the area at the bottom of Internet Explorer is called the command bar when it appears alone. The Weather app (see Chapter 2) has an app bar at the top of the screen and another app bar at the bottom. Computer terminology is tricky.

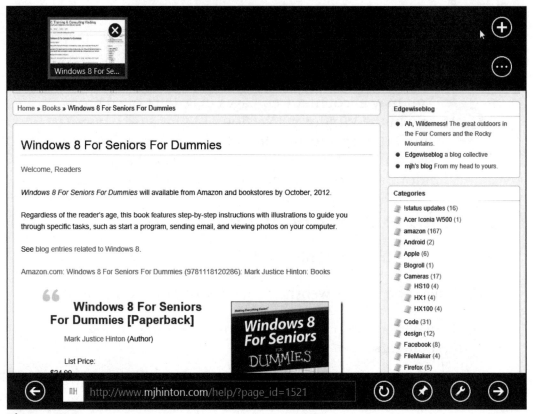

Figure 6-5

4. In the app bar at the top, select the plus sign. On the next screen, select any tile or type a new page address.

5. Display the app bar again. Note two (or more) thumbnails at the top of the screen (see **Figure 6-6**). These are called *tabs*, because older web browsers display notebook-like tabs instead of thumbnails. Select the first thumbnail tab to switch back to the first web page.

> Browsing in multiple tabs allows you to keep one page open while visiting another, perhaps to compare information or to follow a different thought.

> The keyboard shortcut for switching between tabs is Ctrl+Tab.

Figure 6-6

6. Once again, display the app bar. Select the X in the top-right corner of one of the thumbnails to close that particular tab. Close as many open tabs as you want to reduce clutter and to simplify switching between open tabs.

> The keyboard shortcut for closing the current tab is Ctrl+W. (*W*? Long story.)

> When you switch to the Start screen, the pages you are browsing remain open in IE. When you switch back to IE, those pages are ready to use. To start IE fresh without any open pages, close each open tab.

Search for Anything

1. With Internet Explorer open, select the address box and then type **travel**. IE attempts to match what you type with a tile for a page you have browsed. (Ignore these matching tiles for this exercise, but take advantage of them later.) Select the go arrow next to the address box or press Enter.

2. A search results page appears, as shown in **Figure 6-7**. The results come from www.bing.com, which is the default search engine for IE. A *search engine* is simply a website that provides links to web pages that match your search. (That definition, however, ignores the complex process going on behind the scenes.)

 Although you don't have to browse www.bing.com to begin a search, you should browse that page eventually to see the beautiful photos, which change daily (refer to **Figure 6-1**).

3. Scroll down the page of search results. Select any link you want to follow. If you get to the bottom of the page, select Next to see more search results.

4. Return to the search screen using one of the following methods:

- Select the back arrow (or press Alt+left arrow) to return to the previous page. The more pages you've browsed one after another, the less effective the back arrow is in returning to the first page.

- Select the address box. Then either select the Bing tile (if there is one) or type **bing** and select Bing from the matching tiles. The more complex your search, the less effective this method because you have to perform the search repeatedly.

Search results

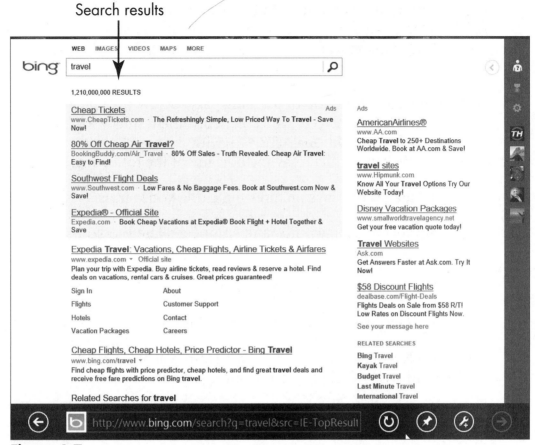

Figure 6-7

5. Select the search box at the top of the Bing page. After the word *travel*, type **new mexico** (no capitals needed). As you type, potential matches for your terms appear directly below the box. If you see an item matching the search you want, select the item. Otherwise, select the magnifying glass button to the right of the box to search.

Different search engines may turn up different results. Other search engines include Google (www.google.com), Ask (www.ask.com), and Yahoo! (www.yahoo.com). To use one of these search engines when exploring the Web, enter its address in the address box.

Search results often include links to suggestions for related searches and a history of recent searches you've made. Take advantage of anything that requires less typing.

6. Note the tabs at the top of the Bing page, below the search box. The first tab is Web, which contains the results you see by default. Additional tabs vary with the search. Select each of the tabs, which may include any of the following:

- **Images** displays pictures matching your terms.

- **Videos** displays clips and snippets related to your search terms.

- **Maps** will help you get there.

- **Places** displays details about a location.

- **News** displays search results from recent news, instead of all the results of the broader Web.

- **More** leads to shopping and services Bing provides, as well as some information on using Bing.

 The Image tab includes the SafeSearch setting, near the top of the page. Your options are Moderate, which attempts to filter out potentially offensive or obscene images, Strict, for even more filtering, and Off, for anything goes.

7. Close IE with one of the following techniques:

- **Mouse:** Move the pointer to the top of the screen until the pointer becomes a hand. Then click and drag IE off the bottom of the screen.

- **Touchscreen:** Swipe from the top edge and drag IE off the bottom of the screen.

- **Keyboard:** Press Alt+F4.

Closing IE or any other app is optional.

 Search the Microsoft Store for the Bing app, which displays results differently and can be snapped to one side of the screen (if your screen supports that). See Chapter 9 for information on using the Microsoft Store.

Work with the Reader App

1. On the Start screen, select the Internet Explorer tile. Then browse the book's web page, at `http://www.win8 mjh.com`. Select the Welcome Readers link.

2. On the Welcome, Reader page, select the link This Document Opens in the Reader App. You see the following message at the bottom of the page (see **Figure 6-8**): *Do you want to open or save reader.pdf from www.mjhinton.com?*.

Select Open to view the document in Reader

Figure 6-8

3. Select Open. The Reader app opens with the contents of the linked document (in a format called PDF). Adobe Acrobat Reader is a program more commonly used to open these documents on computers other than Windows 8.

 Select Save (refer to **Figure 6-8**) if you want to read this document again. By saving the document to your computer, you can open it anytime, without returning to the web page.

4. In Reader, display the app bar, which is shown in **Figure 6-9**. Select the Two Pages button to display two pages at once. Select One Page to see just one page at a time. Continuous (the default option) displays the largest size text and less than one page at a time. Use one of the following methods to display the app bar in any app:

- **Mouse:** Click the right mouse button.

- **Touchscreen:** Swipe down from the top or up from the bottom of the screen.

- **Keyboard:** Press ⊞+Z.

Reader app bar

Figure 6-9

5. In the Reader app bar, select Find, which enables you to search a document for text. Type **reader** and then select the magnifying glass or press the Enter key. Every instance of matching text is highlighted, as shown in **Figure 6-10**. Select Next or Previous to move through the document. Select Results to display a list of matching items in context (useful for long documents). Select Close to end the search.

6. Display the app bar again, and then select Save As. The Files screen appears. Keep or change the filename at the bottom of the screen. Select Save. Saving the document allows you to access it later without browsing the original web page.

 When saving any file, you can select the Files heading for a list of specific locations. If you see SkyDrive, select that to store this file in the cloud (on the Web) and automatically copy it to any linked computers.

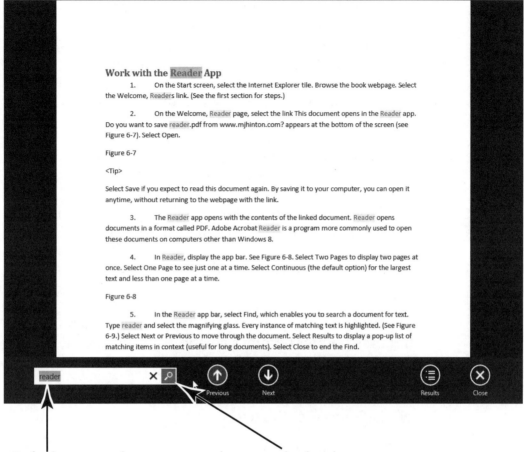

To find text in a document, type here...and select here

Figure 6-10

7. Display the app bar again, and then select Open. A thumbnail of the file you just saved appears, along with an option to browse your computer for other documents. (The current document won't appear because it's already open.) Select the back arrow to return to the open document.

8. Display the app bar one more time, and then select More, which displays the following functions:

- **Rotate** is useful if the document is not rotated correctly.

- **Info** displays information about the document, including who created it and when, as well as the document length. Permissions indicate what functions are available, most importantly printing.

9. To print this document, display the charms bar and then select the Devices charm. In the Devices panel, select your printer. Select the Print button to print or select anything outside the Devices panel to cancel. For information on installing (and using) a printer, see Chapter 13.

 Some documents are quite long, requiring more than one page of paper. Be certain you want to print.

10. Close the Reader app with one of the following techniques:

- **Mouse:** Move the pointer to the top of the screen until the pointer becomes a hand. Then click and drag IE off the bottom of the screen.

- **Touchscreen:** Swipe from the top edge and drag IE off the bottom of the screen.

- **Keyboard:** Press Alt+F4.

Change Microsoft Internet Explorer Settings

1. In Microsoft Internet Explorer, display the charms bar and then select Settings.

2. In the Settings panel for Internet Explorer, select the Internet Options function at the top.

3. Note the option to Delete Browsing History in **Figure 6-11**. Some people delete history for privacy reasons. Be aware that doing so may make using some websites less convenient, specifically sites that recognize you, such as a shopping site.

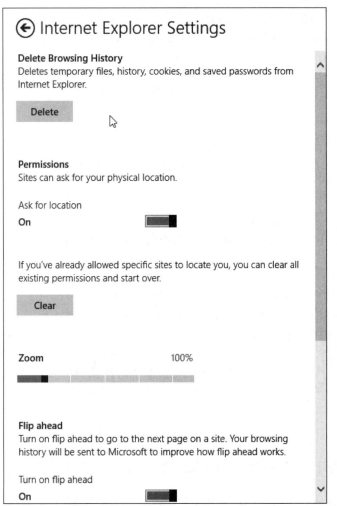

Figure 6-11

4. In the Zoom section, select a spot in the bar. The farther left you select, the more of the page you see and the smaller the text. The farther to the right you select, the less of the page you see and the larger the contents. Notice the changes to the page you were on when you started these steps. Zoom to 120% for improved ease of reading. Select the back arrow at the top of the Settings panel.

5. In the Internet Explorer Settings panel, select Help. Microsoft's help page for Internet Explorer appears in a new tab. Browse the site.

6. On any web page, use one of these methods to change the zoom level:

- **Mouse:** Press the Ctrl key while rolling the mouse wheel away and back, which zooms in and then out.

- **Touchscreen:** Touch two fingers on the screen. Spread your fingers to zoom in. Pinch your fingers to zoom out.

- **Keyboard:** Press Ctrl+plus sign to zoom in. Press Ctrl+minus sign to zoom out. Press Ctrl+0 to return to normal (usually 100 percent).

These methods are independent of the Zoom setting you chose in Step 4, which sets the default zoom level for all pages.

Use Internet Explorer on the Desktop

1. On the Start screen, select the Internet Explorer tile. Select the address box. On the Frequent and Pinned page, select the Windows 8 for Seniors tile, if there is one, or type www.win8mjh.com in the address box and then select the go arrow. The book's website appears.

2. In the command bar at the bottom of the screen, select the page tools (wrench) button to display the menu choices shown in **Figure 6-12**.

 The Find on Page function enables you to type text to search for on the current page.

Get app for this site

Find on page

View on the desktop

Figure 6-12

 A plus sign on the Page Tools button indicates the site has an associated app. If you see Get App for This Site, you can use that option to switch to Microsoft Store for a related app. After the app is installed, you may see Switch to [this site's] App. Consider getting apps that are linked to your most important sites, such as the Bing app.

3. Select View on the Desktop to open the current page in the desktop version of IE, as shown in **Figure 6-13**. See Chapter 5 for help on working with the desktop.

 The desktop version of IE has more functions than the Windows 8 version, including a function called Favorites for organizing your most-visited web pages into folders. Desktop IE also enables you to install more functions called accelerators and add-ons, such as Adobe Reader (for printed documents and forms). If a page refuses to open or looks wrong in the IE app, see if using View on the Desktop helps. Desktop IE may ask for your permission to open or download additional functions. Be careful. Don't accept just anything from any website.

4. Examine the desktop version of IE, which is quite different from the IE app. The address bar at the top of the window displays the web address for the page currently shown in the browser. A tab appears to the right with the title of the page. Additional tabs would appear farther to the right.

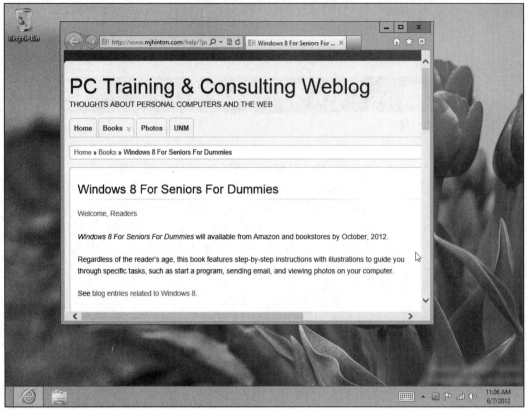

Figure 6-13

 Two keyboard-only shortcuts: To browse the first page listed as you type, press Shift+Enter. For a Web address that begins with www. and ends with .com, such as www.win8mjh.com, you can type just the middle part of the address — for this example, **win8mjh** — and then press Ctrl+Enter. The browser adds the beginning and the end of the address.

5. Scroll the page using one of these methods:

- **Mouse:** Click in the scroll bar area on the right edge of the window. Or roll the mouse wheel toward you or away.

- **Touchscreen:** Drag the page up or down.

- **Keyboard:** Press Page Down or the spacebar. Scroll back up by pressing Page Up or Shift+spacebar. Use the up or down arrows to scroll up or down, respectively, one line at a time.

6. Select the Welcome, Readers link with a click or a tap.

 A web page may take some time to open. Look in the tab for indications of a delay, such as a *Wait* message or a rotating circle.

7. To return to the preceding page, select the back arrow to the left of the address bar or press Alt+left arrow or the Backspace key.

8. To go to the Welcome page again, select the forward arrow (or press Alt+right arrow). The browser remembers the pages you visit to make it easy to go forward and back.

9. Switch to the Start screen using one of the following methods:

- **Mouse:** Move the pointer to the lower-left corner of the screen, and then click.

- **Touchscreen:** Swipe from the right edge for the charms bar, and then tap the Start charm.

- **Keyboard:** Press the ▦ key.

 You can use the desktop version of Internet Explorer also by selecting the Desktop tile on the Start screen. Then start Microsoft Internet Explorer (IE) by selecting the blue *e* icon in the taskbar at the bottom of the screen.

E-Mailing Family and Friends

E-mail has largely replaced the notes and letters of previous centuries. Every day, billions of e-mail messages circle the globe, conveying greetings, news, jokes, even condolences.

E-mail also provides a way to send and receive *attachments*, such as documents or photos. Who needs faxes or postcards?

The Mail app gives you access to e-mail using your Microsoft Account. A glance at the Start screen can tell you whether you have unread e-mail and if so, who it is from.

Your Microsoft Account can be associated with an e-mail address from any e-mail service provider, including Microsoft's own Hotmail (www.hotmail.com), Live (www.live.com), Outlook (www.outlook.com) or Xbox (www.xbox.com). You can also use e-mail services such as Yahoo (www.yahoo.com) and Gmail (www.gmail.com) without having a Microsoft Account. However, you have to access non–Microsoft Account e-mail using a web browser or an app other than Microsoft's Mail app. See Chapter 6 for information on browsing the Web.

In this chapter, you use the Mail app for e-mail. You compose, format, and send e-mail, as well as respond to incoming e-mail.

 If you don't have a physical keyboard, see Chapter 1 for information on using the virtual keyboard.

Use the Mail App

1. For e-mail on Windows 8, select the Mail tile on the Start screen. If you are not currently signed in using a Microsoft Account, enter your e-mail address and password on the Sign In screen that appears, and then select Sign In. (See Chapter 4 for information on creating a Microsoft Account.)

2. The first time you use the Mail app, you may not see much, if you haven't used your Microsoft Account for e-mail on another computer. Who would have written you already? You may, however, see a message or two from Microsoft.

3. On the Inbox screen, select the back arrow in the upper-left corner. ("Back" seems odd given that you haven't been to the screen you're about to see. Computers aren't as consistent as people believe.) The Mail panel slides in from the left, replacing the Inbox panel, as shown in **Figure 7-1**.

 If the screen resolution is high enough to allow more information on the screen, you may see the Mail panel and the Inbox panel side-by-side. At lower resolutions, these panels replace each other as you choose them.

4. Select any of the following categories in the Mail panel, and then use the back arrow to return to the Mail panel:

- **Inbox:** E-mail you have received but not moved elsewhere appears here, including both read and unread e-mail.

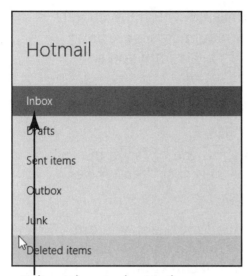

Select Inbox in the Mail pane

Figure 7-1

- **Drafts:** As you compose e-mail (next section), you can save your message as a draft until you are ready to send it.

- **Sent Items:** Copies of the e-mail you send are stored here, appropriately.

- **Outbox:** When you send e-mail, it moves to the Outbox until it has been processed, which may be instantaneously. If you're not connected to the Internet, e-mail waits here until you establish a connection, and then it is sent.

- **Junk:** Messages are moved here — either automatically or by you — instead of the Inbox, if they are suspected of being, well, *junk*. The more common term for unwanted e-mail is *spam*. (It's a long story.) You may want to check this folder occasionally to see if a message was misfiled here.

- **Deleted Items:** Self-explanatory? You can move messages out of Deleted Items if you change your mind.

As you switch categories, Mail syncs with the Web to display items in that category. You may not see anything other than *Syncing* or *Up to date* until you send and receive e-mail.

5. Proceed to the next section, "Write an E-Mail Message."

 You can say "send me e-mail," instead of "send me an e-mail message." I, for one, never say "send me *an* e-mail."

 After you've received some e-mail messages, you can search for specific messages by displaying the charms bar, selecting Search, and then selecting Mail and typing the content you're searching for in the search box, such as subject, sender, or something in the message. This process works anywhere — you don't have to be in the Mail app.

Write an E-Mail Message

1. To compose an e-mail message in the Mail app, select the New button (it looks like a plus sign) in the upper-right corner of the screen. (It doesn't matter which panel appears on the left.) The Compose screen appears, as shown in **Figure 7-2**.

Enter an e-mail address

mark hinton	Add a subject	(=☑) (✕)
markjusticehinton@hotmail...		
To	Add a message	
[ ] ⊕	Sent from Windows Mail	
Cc		
[ ] ⊕		
Show more		

Figure 7-2

2. Note your name and e-mail address above the To box. This is the information your e-mail recipient will see in his or her e-mail app as the Sender or From line.

3. In the To box, type an e-mail address. (Feel free to write me using `markjusticehinton@hotmail.com`.) If the e-mail address is incomplete, it will be highlighted in a red box. Press the Tab key, touch the screen, or use the mouse to move to the next option.

 Instead of typing an address, you can use the plus sign next to the To box to select contacts from the People app (Windows 8's address book), but you probably don't have any contacts at this time. See Chapter 8 for information on adding contacts to the People app.

 To send e-mail to more than one person at once, press Enter after you type an address. The To box expands for another e-mail address. You can also enter an e-mail address in the CC box. (Once upon a time, *CC* stood for *carbon copy*, and then it became *courtesy copy*.) Technically, it makes no difference whether you use additional To addresses or the CC. To send a copy without revealing you've done so, select Show More, and then enter addresses in the BCC (*blind* or *blocked* CC).

4. Select the box that displays Add a Subject (that prompt disappears when you select the box). Enter a few words describing your message content or purpose. Using lowercase is fine.

5. Select below the Subject line. Type your message. Avoid all caps — purists consider caps to be SHOUTING! No need to press Enter as you approach the end of the line — this isn't a typewriter.

Some people start a message with a salutation, such as *Hi, Mark*, but many people do not. Some people sign e-mail using their initials. E-mail can be as formal or casual as you choose to make it.

 Words underlined with a red squiggle aren't recognized by Windows 8 and may be misspelled. Right-click or tap and hold to see a pop-up list of suggested spellings. If the spelling is correct, use Add to Dictionary for words you use frequently or Ignore for those you don't.

6. When you're ready to send the message, select the Send button, which looks like an envelope. If you aren't ready to send the message, select the Close button (an *X*) and then choose either Save Draft or Delete, depending on whether or not you want to continue with this message at another time.

 Not surprisingly, you can select the Drafts category in the Mail panel to see a message you saved as a draft. To resume editing, select the message there. Then you can send the message or save it again.

7. If you select the Send button, your message is sent and you return to the screen you were on at the beginning of Step 1.

8. Repeat from Step 1 as needed.

Format E-Mail

1. If you want to add bold, italics, even color to e-mail, select the text you want to fancy-up. If no text is selected, your formatting will apply to the word in which the *cursor* (the blinking vertical line in the content) is located.

- **Mouse:** Click and drag the mouse pointer over the text you want to select.

- **Touchscreen:** Tap and drag over the text you want to select.

- **Keyboard:** With the cursor at the beginning of the text you want to select, hold down the Shift key as you press the right or down arrow to select text. Release the Shift key only after you have completed your selection.

 To apply formatting to one word, double-click or double-tap that word to select it and display the app bar in one step.

 The keyboard shortcut to select all text is Ctrl+A. No mouse or touchscreen method is quite so complete.

2. The formatting app bar appears as you make your selection, as shown in **Figure 7-3.** Select any of the following formatting options:

- **Font:** Choose a font by name and specify the size of the text. For example, the text in this book is Giovinni Book and the font size is 12.5. The older I get, the larger the font I use.

- **Bold:** Bold is used for emphasis to make text stand out.

- **Italic:** Although italic can also be used for emphasis, it may be harder to read than normal or bold text.

- **Underline:** Because links are usually underlined automatically, you may want to avoid underlining text that isn't a link.

- **Text Color:** Choose from the colors that pop up when you select this option.

- **Emoticons:** This option opens a panel on the left. The top row of choices changes the *emoticons* (smiley faces and other small pictures or symbols) available in the panel. Choices are Recently Used, People and Faces, Activities, Food and Things, Travel, Nature, and Symbols. These options could keep you busy for days.

 See Chapter 1 for information on using the virtual keyboard's emoticons.

- **More:** This button displays four more options: Bulleted List (like this one), Numbered List, Undo, and Redo.

 The keyboard shortcut for Undo is Ctrl+Z. For Redo, press Ctrl+Y.

Select text to format

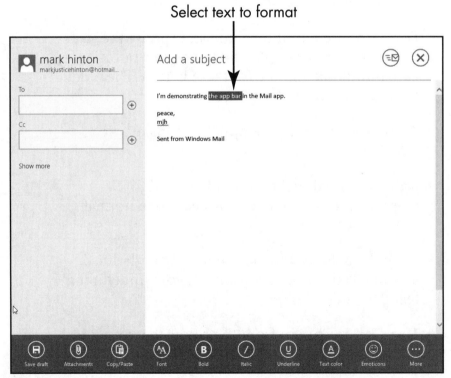

Figure 7-3

The Attachments option opens the *file picker*, which lets you select documents and photos. When the file picker appears, select a file to attach or select the Files heading to navigate to other locations or apps, such as Camera and SkyDrive.

3. When you have finished formatting the text, select the Send button.

Read and Respond to Incoming E-Mail

1. On the Start screen, you may see an indication that you have received e-mail. Note that the Mail tile may display the following information:

- The wide, rectangular tile displays the sender's address or name, the subject line, and a portion of each unread message in succession, as well as a count of unread messages.

- The small, square tile displays the unread message count.

- Small or wide, the tile doesn't display any information if the Live Tile option is off.

2. Select the Mail tile. The Mail app opens on the last screen you viewed — not on the specific message displayed on the live tile, if any.

3. If necessary, select Inbox from the Mail panel. See the section "Use the Mail App" for the steps. Unread messages appear in bold.

4. Select a message under the Inbox heading. The content of that message appears to the right, as shown in **Figure 7-4**.

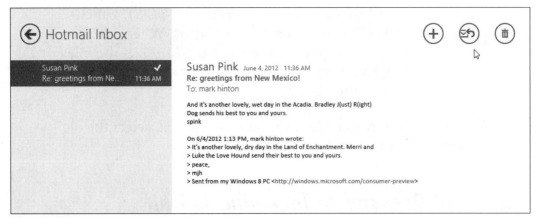

Figure 7-4

5. After you read the message, you can select one of the following options in the upper-right corner:

- The **New** button (the plus sign) starts a new message to anyone.

- The **Respond** button (with an arrow curving back on an envelope) creates a new message based on the current message.

- The **Delete** button (the trash can) moves the e-mail from Inbox to Deleted Items.

6. Select the Respond button, and then Select Reply from the list that appears. Reply starts a new message (refer to **Figure 7-2**) in response to the selected message and includes the text of the selected message. The subject line is automatically *Re: [the original subject]*. You'll use this option most often. Complete your message and select the Send button.

 In the Respond button list, Reply All sends your response to all the other recipients, if a message is addressed to more than one person. The Reply option sends your response only to the sender. Select Forward to send the selected message to someone else. You can add your own text or remove portions of the forwarded message in the process.

See the sections "Write an E-Mail Message" and "Format E-Mail" for more information on composing an e-mail message.

7. Select any message in the Inbox category. Display the Mail app bar by using a right-click, by swiping up or down, or by pressing ⊞+Z. Note the following options:

- **Move:** Use this option to move the selected e-mail from one category on the left to another. For example, move a message to the Junk category or from Junk to Inbox, if it's a message you want. When you select Move, the screen appears slightly dimmed. In the Mail panel, select the category to which you want to move the selected e-mail. Categories that disappear during a move are unavailable. If you select Move but don't want to continue, cancel by double-clicking or double-tapping in the message content area or by pressing the Esc key.

- **Pin to Start:** Use this option to create a new tile for the specific category on the screen (in this case, Inbox). This tile takes you directly to the selected category (not the selected message). Selecting the original Mail tile takes you to the last screen you viewed. The Pin to Start option is a good one to use with Inbox. When you select Pin to Start, a box pops up. You can change the text that will be displayed on the new tile or not, and then select the Pin to Start button.

- **Mark Unread:** Use this option if you want the message to appear unread (bold in Inbox). Some people do this with messages they want to deal with later.

- **Sync:** Mail syncs with the Web automatically. However, if you think Mail is out of sync, use this option.

You don't have to do anything with e-mail in the Inbox category. Instead, you can read other messages, use the back arrow to select a different category, or switch away from the Mail app to the Start screen. If you let unread e-mail accumulate in your inbox, however, you'll only have more to deal with later.

 If you add e-mail accounts from providers such as Gmail, you may see additional categories or options. See the section "Add an E-Mail Account" at the end of the chapter.

Send E-Mail from Other Apps

1. You can e-mail information from other apps, such as Internet Explorer and News. On the Start screen, select the Internet Explorer tile. See Chapter 6 for information on using the web browser. Enter the web address for the book: **www.win8mjh.com**.

2. On any web page, display the Share panel using one of the following methods:

  • **Mouse:** Move the mouse pointer to the upper-right corner of the screen. On the charms bar, select the Share charm.

  • **Touchscreen:** Swipe from the right edge of the screen, and then tap the Share charm.

  • **Keyboard:** Press ⊞+H (think *sHare*) to go straight to the Share panel.

3. On the Share panel, shown in **Figure 7-5,** select the Mail tile.

Figure 7-5

 Mail isn't available for sharing with all apps. You won't know until you try.

4. The Mail panel slides in from the right, as shown in **Figure 7-6.** Enter an e-mail address under To. The subject line is automatically the title of the web page, but you can change the subject. A thumbnail image of the web page, as well as the site name and address, appear in the content area. You can add, delete, or change any of this. When you are ready to send the message, select the Send button.

Curiously, formatting options aren't available in this panel, except as keyboard shortcuts such as Ctrl+B for bold, Ctrl+I for italic, and Ctrl+U for underline. Repeating the keyboard shortcut removes the formatting. The Delete and Save to Drafts options are also missing here. To cancel this e-mail, select the back arrow next to Mail or select anywhere outside the panel.

The next time you use the Share panel in Internet Explorer or another app that shares with Mail, the e-mail address you used in Step 4 appears near the top of the panel. Select that address to save time in sharing something else with that person.

Figure 7-6

Change Mail Settings

1. In Mail, display the Settings panel, shown in **Figure** 7-7. Then select Accounts.

2. On the Accounts panel, select your e-mail account at the top of the panel. Note these settings, which are shown in **Figure** 7-8:

  • **Account Name:** The name of the e-mail service provider. You can change this, if you want. I might use *Mark's e-mail.*

  • **Download New Email:** If you don't want e-mail constantly streaming into Inbox, you can change this setting to every 15 or 30 minutes, Hourly, or Manual, in which case use the Sync button on the Mail app bar to check your mail.

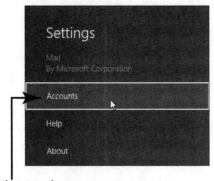

The Mail app can access
multiple e-mail accounts
Figure 7-7

- **Download Email From:** You can limit how far
  back to download messages to your computer.
  This setting isn't relevant in a new e-mail account.

- **Content to Sync:** Understandably, you want to
  sync e-mail between your service provider and
  your computer. However, you may see options to
  sync Contacts, Calendar, or other information
  between the service provider and your computer.
  Generally, you want everything in sync.

- **Automatically Download External Images:** By
  default, Mail downloads images attached to or
  embedded in e-mail messages. Turn off this option
  to avoid downloading images, if you're paying for
  your Internet connection by the minute or byte.

- **Use an Email Signature:** Mail automatically inserts
  Sent from Windows Mail into each message. Enter
  text here that you want automatically inserted at the
  end of your message. For example, I use *peace, mjh*
  as my e-mail signature. If you don't want any text
  inserted automatically, select the switch under this
  option to change it from Yes to No.

- **Email Address:** This setting is a reminder of your
  e-mail address.

- **Show Email Notifications for This Account:** Turn on this setting to see pop-up notifications when new e-mail arrives.

- **Remove This Account or Remove All Accounts:** If you don't want to receive e-mail from a specific account, you can remove it from this computer. Doing so has no effect on the account itself, which you can still access through a web browser or by adding the account to Mail or another app.

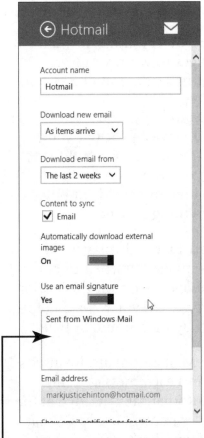

Enter text to automatically add e-mail

Figure 7-8

Add an E-Mail Account to Mail

1. If you have another e-mail address, you can add it to Mail. For example, follow these steps to add an existing Gmail account to Mail. In Mail, display the Settings panel (refer to **Figure 7-7**) and then select Accounts.

2. In the Accounts panel, select Add an Account.

 Many people have more than one e-mail address. Your Internet service provider probably gave you an e-mail account and you may have another through work or school. However, this feature isn't for everyone.

3. In the Add an Account panel, select the service with which you have an e-mail account. If your service doesn't appear here, select Other Account. If you have a Gmail address (or you just want to see what's next), select Google.

4. On the Add Your Google Account screen, enter your Gmail address and password in the appropriate boxes. Select Include Your Google Contacts and Calendars, and then select Connect. Cancel if you don't want to continue.

5. You may see the messages *Adding your account* and then *Syncing*. If you don't see the account, display the Mail panel, if necessary, using the back arrow, and then select Gmail at the bottom of the Mail panel. In **Figure 7-9**, my Gmail Inbox has one unread message. To see that message, I would select the Inbox. I can select Hotmail rather than Gmail, depending on which I want to use.

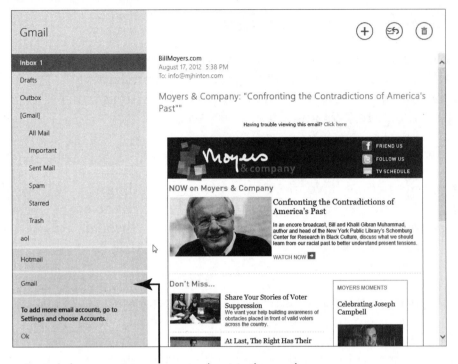

Switch between accounts in the Mail panel

Figure 7-9

 Gmail uses *labels* you create to organize e-mail. Other services use *folders* instead of labels. When Gmail is selected, I see its labels, starting with All Mail, below the standard Mail categories. You may encounter other features supported by one e-mail service but not another.

 See the preceding section, "Change Mail Settings," for the steps to review or change settings for your newly added account.

Staying in Touch with People

*T*he Web brings people together in many ways beyond e-mail. Long ago, paleo-nerds hunkered in bulletin board systems, precursors to today's forums. *Social networks* are digital neighborhoods where your neighbors include family, friends, colleagues — maybe even your real neighbors. We use social networks to *share* the information or entertainment we discover and to post *status updates*, short declarations of the moment, such as *I'm feeling particularly eloquent today.*

Unlike the broader Web, these social networks are gated communities that require an account name and password for full access. This suggestion of privacy and security, however, shouldn't be completely trusted. If nothing else, the networks themselves are watching you.

A few social networks are worth noting here: Facebook, Twitter, and Flickr. You find out more about these and others shortly. For now, realize that each social network is a separate website with its own way of doing things, requiring some mental adjustment as you move between them. Furthermore, how a site works may change from one visit to the next, often to the dismay of participants. Moreover, with so many people posting so many thoughts, links, and likes, keeping up becomes a problem.

The People app comes to your rescue by pulling in contact information, status updates, and more from several services at once. Use the People app as your address book and as a window on what everyone is doing without having to navigate through each network's website.

In this chapter, you add contacts to the People app, both manually and by connecting to Facebook or another service. You make your most important contacts stand out by pinning them to the Start screen or marking them as *favorites*, for prominence in the People app. You use the Messaging app to chat (in text) with contacts. (*Chat*, which is also called instant messaging, is a more immediate back-and-forth communication than e-mail.) Finally, you use the Calendar app to keep track of birthdays, anniversaries, appointments, and other events.

Explore the Social Networks

If you don't have an account with Facebook or another social network, you can create an account through the People app. However, I recommend that you go to a service's website to create a new account, and then use your new account name and password in the People app.

➡ **Facebook** (www.facebook.com) is the epitome of social networks. You know about Facebook already, unless you've been living in a cave. (These days, even caves have Internet connections.) Billions of people and organizations have Facebook accounts and *pages*. Facebook popularized the verbification of *friend* (bow your head for the late *befriend*), as well as the use of *like* as a mere acknowledgment, a tip of the hat, if you will. (The less popular *hat tip* or *ht* is a favorite among *bloggers*, digital journal-keepers who stand apart from the collective.) Somehow *poke* as a greeting hasn't gained the same traction as other new usages.

➡ **Twitter** (www.twitter.com) pares communication down to short status updates (*tweets*) in an endless stream of text messages. Twitter is favored by professional journalists and bumper-sticker fans.

➡ **LinkedIn** (www.linkedin.com) is popular among professionals seeking business contacts (and jobs) more than casual social interaction.

➡ **Flickr** (www.flickr.com) is older than the upstarts and immensely popular among photographers and lovers of photography.

➡ **Pinterest** (www.pinterest.com) has quickly collected enthusiasts who share images in shifting mosaics.

➡ **MySpace** (www.myspace.com) lost the race to Facebook and serves as a reminder that, like empires, social networks do not endure. It is our need to connect that endures.

Add Contacts to the People App

1. On the Start screen, select the People app.

2. If you haven't signed in already using your Microsoft Account, the Sign In screen appears. Enter your Microsoft Account e-mail address and password, and then select Sign In.

 You need a Microsoft Account to use Mail, Calendar, People, or Messaging. When you sign in to one, you're signed in to all four apps. See Chapter 4 for information on creating a Microsoft Account.

3. What you see first in People depends on whether the app found contact information associated with your Microsoft Account. You may see familiar names or an invitation to connect to other services. For now, add one new contact manually. (You connect to other services later.) Display the New Contact screen by selecting the New button on the People app bar (see **Figure 8-1**), using one of the following methods:

- **Mouse:** Click the right mouse button. Click the New button, which sports a plus sign.

- **Touchscreen:** Swipe down from the top or up from the bottom of the screen. Tap New (the plus sign).

- **Keyboard:** Press ⊞+Z. Press the Tab key until New (the plus sign) is highlighted, and then press the Enter key.

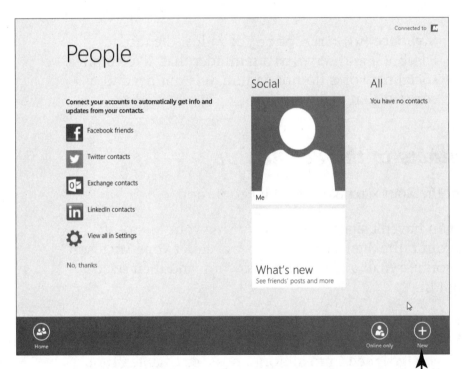

Select New to add someone to your address book

Figure 8-1

4. Much of the information on the New Contact screen (shown in **Figure 8-2**) is optional. Enter the information that you want access to throughout Windows 8, not just in the People app. (For example, think about what you want to access in Mail.) You can enter any person's name and information you want, but let me suggest the following:

- **Account:** Ultimately, you may link multiple accounts using the People app. Which account do you want this new contact associated with? For now, only one option may be available.

- **First Name: Mark.**

- **Last Name: Hinton.**

- **Company: PC Training & Consulting.**

- **Email: markjusticehinton@hotmail.com.** (Select Personal and choose Work from the pop-up list.)

- **Phone:** (Leave phone blank for me.) Select Mobile and note the many categories for phone numbers.

Enter just the information you want

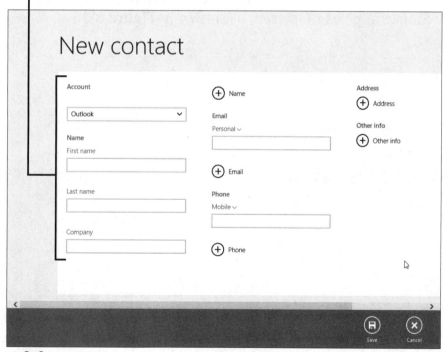

Figure 8-2

5. Note the following buttons with plus signs. Select each in turn to see the available options. Add data as you want:

- **Name:** You can add a middle name (**Justice**), nickname (**mjh**), title (**Computerist**), as well as several other names.

- **Email:** Add up to two more e-mail addresses.

- **Phone:** Add up to seven more phone numbers!

- **Address:** Add up to three mailing addresses.

- **Other Info:** Options include Job Title (**Author**), Significant Other (**Merri**), Website (**www.win8 mjh.com**), and Notes, a box for free-form notes.

6. When you're done, select Save to add this contact (or select Cancel to throw away the new contact). The added contact appears on-screen, as shown in **Figure 8-3**.

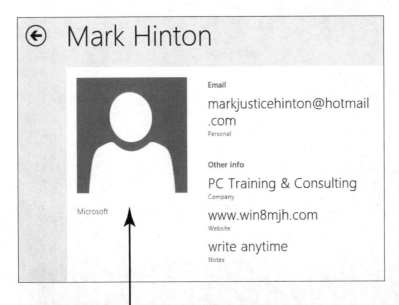

Information on the contact card
Figure 8-3

7. Select People in the app bar or select the back arrow.

 The photo associated with a contact is usually selected by the contact as part of his or her profile on a specific network. The generic image in **Figure 8-3** may change as you connect to social networks.

Connect to Social Networks

1. In the preceding section, you added one contact. For access to all your contacts from another service, such as Facebook, display the Settings panel in the People app. See Chapter 2 for information on accessing an app's settings.

 The very first time you use the People app, you may see an option to connect to other services. You could start there and jump to Step 4 in this section.

2. On the Settings panel, select Accounts.

 For an account you've already added, select that account in the Accounts panel to configure what data Windows 8 downloads and how frequently the downloads occur.

3. In the Accounts panel (see **Figure 8-4**), select Add an Account.

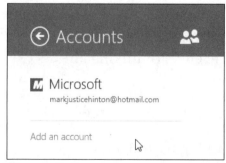

Figure 8-4

4. In the Add an Account panel, select Facebook, unless you don't have a Facebook account. (Let me shake your hand, you rare creature.) You can choose another service, in which case the steps will be similar but the screens will be different.

5. The screen briefly displays *Connecting to a Service*, and then the Connect screen appears. If you see What Else Happens When I Connect, select that option to read everything that will happen, as shown in **Figure 8-5.**

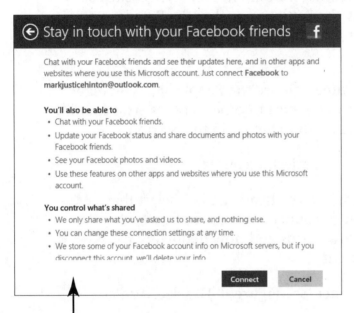

<< Stay in touch with your Facebook friends   f

Chat with your Facebook friends and see their updates here, and in other apps and websites where you use this Microsoft account. Just connect **Facebook** to **markjusticehinton@outlook.com**.

You'll also be able to
- Chat with your Facebook friends.
- Update your Facebook status and share documents and photos with your Facebook friends.
- See your Facebook photos and videos.
- Use these features on other apps and websites where you use this Microsoft account.

You control what's shared
- We only share what you've asked us to share, and nothing else.
- You can change these connection settings at any time.
- We store some of your Facebook account info on Microsoft servers, but if you disconnect this account, we'll delete your info.

Connect   Cancel

Read the details before you select Connect

Figure 8-5

 Understandably, most people are concerned about privacy. We don't know fully the effect of linking all our activity on the Web.

6. Select the Connect button. Or select Cancel, if you prefer.

7. On the Connecting screen, shown in **Figure 8-6,** enter your e-mail address and password (or other account information for the selected service). Select Keep Me

Logged In or Remember Me for convenience. Then select the Log In or Authorize button. (The wording of buttons varies with the service but the underlying choice is Yes or No.)

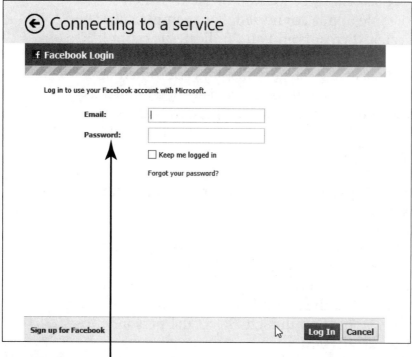

Enter your account information

Figure 8-6

8. The service you're connecting to may display additional forms or information. Facebook displays the Name New Device screen, which refers to your computer. The name you enter here appears in an e-mail message from Facebook as a security measure to confirm that you're the one signing in. Enter a name you'll recognize, and then select Save Device.

9. As the final screen says, you're ready to go. Select Done.

10. After the People app synchronizes with your added
service, the People screen displays all your contacts,
including those from the added service.

 Look for small logos in the upper-right corner of the
People screen; these logos indicate to which services
the People app is connected. For example, an *M*
indicates Microsoft and an *f* indicates Facebook.

 The What's New category displays combined updates
from people on your connected services, much as
you would see on your home page for each service.

Catch Up with People

1. In the People app, select one of your contacts from the
People screen.

 On the People screen, type a letter to begin searching
by name (the Search panel slides in as soon as you
type any letter on the People home screen). Press
Enter or select the magnifying glass button to search.
Matches appear on the left. Select the person whose
contact details you want.

 In apps in which Search doesn't start automatically as
you type, display the charms bar, and then select
Search.

2. The contact screen for the selected person appears, as
shown in **Figure 8-7**. That person's name and profile
photo (or a generic silhouette) appear. Note the following information may appear:

- **Send Message** or **Send Email:** Select this option to
send e-mail (the screen switches to the Mail app) or
a message through the service from the People app.

- **Map Address:** If an address is part of the contact details, select this option to see the location of that address in the Map app.

- **View Profile:** View the contact's service Profile in the web browser (in this case, the contact's Facebook page). Select the down-pointing triangle to the right of View Profile. You may see additional services that the contact uses; select a service if you want to see the contact's profile. Select the More Details option to display in the People app the full address and phone information for the contact.

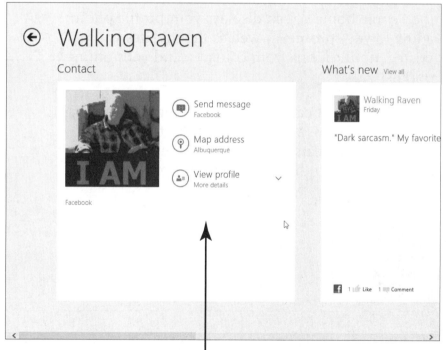

Select an option or scroll right to see more

Figure 8-7

 When you write an e-mail message in the Mail app, you can select recipients from your contacts, instead of manually entering e-mail addresses. See Chapter 7 for information on writing e-mail.

3. Scroll to the right to see additional information, such as the What's New (also called status updates) and Photos sections.

 This contact screen is more than static data. You are looking at the information you would see on the service's own web pages. You can even interact, adding comments and *likes* (the Facebook term for a thumbs-up, or a vote of approval).

4. Select All Updates for even more activity. Select the back arrow to return to the contact's main screen.

 Much like the contact details screen, the Me item on the People home screen displays your profile photo, a link to your profile, as well as the updates you've posted, notifications from contacts, and your online photos.

5. To make this contact easier to access, display the app bar on the contact screen, and then Select Pin to Start. The Pin to Start box appears, as shown in **Figure 8-8.** Change the text or not. Select the Pin to Start button.

Figure 8-8

6. Switch to the Start screen. Scroll to the right to see the tile for the contact you pinned. This live tile displays the contact's profile photo alternating with recent status updates.

See Chapter 2 for information on arranging tiles on the Start screen.

7. Select the contact tile you just pinned. (If necessary, open the People app and select the contact again.) Display the app bar again. Note that the option now reads Unpin from Start.

8. Select Favorite in the app bar (refer to **Figure 8-8**). The app bar disappears. Return to the People screen by redisplaying the app bar and selecting Home. On the People screen, contacts you flag using Favorite appear first, with larger tiles. (You can have as many favorites as you choose.) Select the favorite contact to return to the contact's main screen.

9. Display the app bar for the contact again. Select Edit. The Edit Contact Info screen appears and is largely the same as the New Contact screen (refer to **Figure 8-2**). Select Cancel, unless you change information that you want to save.

Use the Link option on the app bar to consolidate separate contacts. For example, your friend may end up in People as two separate contacts from two separate services. Link the two contacts.

To delete a contact from a connected service, you must go to the website for that service, such as www. facebook.com, and delete the contact there. When the People app syncs with the service, the contact will disappear from the app.

Use the Messaging App to Chat

1. On the Start screen, select the Messaging app. The most recent messages you have received or sent appear on the Messaging home screen.

 The Messaging app connects to the same services as Mail, People, and Calendar. Small logos in the lower-right corner indicate which services are connected. To add or manage accounts, see the section "Connecting to Contacts from Social Networks."

2. Select the New Message button, as shown in **Figure 8-9**.

Select to send a new message

Figure 8-9

3. The People app opens, allowing you to select the contacts to which you want to send an instant message. Select Online Only. (Type a single letter to quickly scroll to a name starting with that letter.) Select as many contacts as you want, and then select the Choose button.

 Although you'll see options for All and Online Only in the People app, sending instant messages to people who are actually online makes the most sense. If you send an instant message to people who are offline, they see it later when they log in, at which time you may be offline. Use e-mail for people who aren't online.

4. The Messaging screen appears with the selected contacts(s). In the message box, type the message you want to send, and then press Enter.

Select the smiley face to insert symbols or emoticons from a palette that pops up.

5. When your contact replies, the reply will appear below your original message. This sequence is called a *thread*. You two can go back and forth, sending and receiving messages, for quite a while, as shown in **Figure 8-10**.

The exchange of messages in a thread

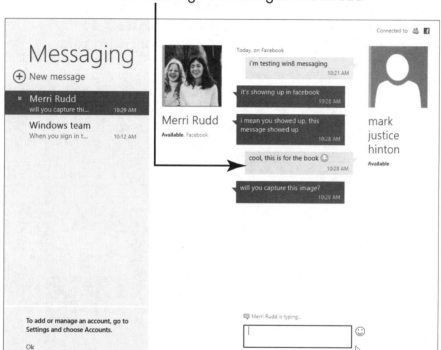

Figure 8-10

 Be patient and give your correspondent time to read and reply. You may see *[contact name] is typing* just above your message box.

6. Return to the Start screen. The Messaging live tile displays incoming messages. Select the tile to open the app and respond.

Face-to-face video chatting is coming to Windows 8. Look for Skype among your installed apps or in the Microsoft Store. Visit the book website (www.win8 mjh.com) for the latest on using the Skype app.

Add a Birthday or Anniversary to the Calendar

1. To see the calendar and add events, open the Calendar app from the Start screen. You may see events and appointments from services you connected to in People or Mail. Display the app bar, as shown in **Figure 8-11,** by using a right-click, by swiping up or down, or by pressing ⊞+Z.

August 2012						
Sunday	Monday	Tuesday	Wednesday	Thursday	Friday	Saturday
29	30	31	1	2	3	4
5	6	7	8	9	10	11
12	13	14	15	16	17	18
19	20	21	22	23	24	25
26	27	28	29	30	31	1

Day   Week   Month   Today   New

Change formats using the Calendar app bar

Figure 8-11

2. On the Calendar app bar, select each of the following familiar formats, redisplaying the app bar each time:

- **Day:** This format displays two days side by side (initially, *Today* and *Tomorrow*), with a box for each hour. Select arrows near the top of the screen to scroll back or forward one day at a time. Scroll up and down to see more hours in the day.

- **Week:** *This week* appears. As with the Day format, scroll up and down to see different hours and use the arrows to move forward or back a week at a time.

- **Month:** The current month appears in the classic month layout. Today is highlighted with a different color. Use arrows near the top to move forward and back a month at a time.

 Select Today from the app bar to return to today from any other date.

3. To create a new event, select any date in the month (or select any hour in the Day or Week formats). The Details screen appears, as shown in **Figure 8-12**.

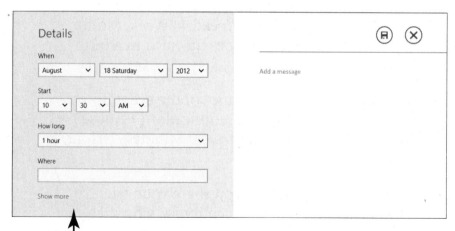

Add information for an event
Figure 8-12

An alternative way to add an event is to select the New button in the app bar.

4. Change any of the following data for an event:

- **When:** Select the month, day, and year from pop-up lists.

- **Start:** Select the hour, minute, and AM or PM from pop-up lists.

- **How Long:** For standard blocks of time, select from 0 Minutes, 30 Minutes, 1 hour, 90 Minutes, or 2 Hours. Select All Day for events that don't have a specific start and stop time. For an end time with the same options as Start, select Custom, and then make an appropriate selection — use this option for multiday events, such as a vacation.

- **Where:** The location of the event, either in general (*downtown*, for example) or a specific location name or address.

 Select Show More for additional options.

- **How Often:** Most events occur once. However, you can select Every Day, Weekday, Week, Month, or Year to create a recurring event, such as a birthday or an anniversary.

- **Reminder:** How far in advance of the event do you want Calendar to display a notification? Choose None, 5 Minutes, 15 Minutes, 30 Minutes, 1 Hour, 1 Day, 18 Hours, or 1 Week.

- **Status:** Use this option if you share your calendar with someone, such as a receptionist, who may schedule you for other events.

- **Who:** Enter one or more e-mail addresses. A copy of the event details will be e-mailed to these addresses. Use Who in lieu of the Share charm.

- **Private:** Select this option to prevent this event from appearing on a shared or public calendar. The event remains visible on your own screen.

5. On the right side of the details screen, enter the event name above the line. Add an optional message or note below the line.

6. When you're done, select the Save button (or Send, if you entered an e-mail address in Who). Or select the Cancel button (*X*) if you don't want to create an event.

7. On the calendar, your event appears on the specified date and time.

8. To edit an event, select it on the calendar. The Details screen opens. Add or change any detail.

 To delete an event, edit it, then select the Delete button (a trash can). If you added the event through a different service, you may have to return to that service to delete the event.

 If your Microsoft Account is connected to services such as Facebook and Gmail, events from those services appear on your calendar. Display the Settings panel, and then select Account to add or remove connected accounts. Display the Settings panel, and then select Options to show or hide connected calendars and to specify different colors for different calendars' events.

Tweak PC Settings for Social Apps

1. Change how the apps in this chapter let you know what's going on. On any screen, display the charms bar, select Settings, and then select Change PC Settings.

 See Chapter 3 for information about the PC Settings options.

2. Select Personalize on the left, and then select Lock Screen on the right if necessary. (Lock Screen probably appears automatically.) Scroll down the right side to the Lock Screen Apps section, as shown in **Figure 8-13**.

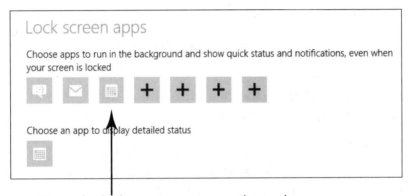

Control which apps appear on the Lock screen

Figure 8-13

3. Some apps can display information on the Lock screen. This information can be brief (in the first row of icons) or detailed (the last icon). In **Figure 8-13**, the first three icons represent Messaging, Mail, and Calendar. Four more positions are available, as represented by the plus signs. To add a fourth app, select one of the plus signs.

To change one of the current apps, select its icon. In either case, the Choose an App pop-up appears listing all apps capable of displaying summary information. For example, Messaging and Mail display the number of unread messages for each app, respectively. Select the app you want from the pop-up, for example, Weather. If you don't want any app in that particular position, select Don't Show Quick Status Here (*here* means this specific position). You can modify any or all of these positions.

4. In the same section, the second row contains a single button that you use for an app for which you want to display more detail. For example, if you choose the Calendar app, your next appointment and all-day events will appear on the Lock screen. Select the icon, and then select the app you want from the Choose an App pop-up. If you don't want any detailed information on the Lock screen, select Don't Show Detailed Status on the Lock Screen.

5. On the left, select Notifications. The screen shown in **Figure 8-14** appears. If you're bothered by notifications popping up, turn off the ones you don't want — for all apps, with the first option, or for individual apps, in the lower section. If the sound that accompanies notifications becomes a problem, turn off the Play Notification Sounds option.

6. Return to the Start screen.

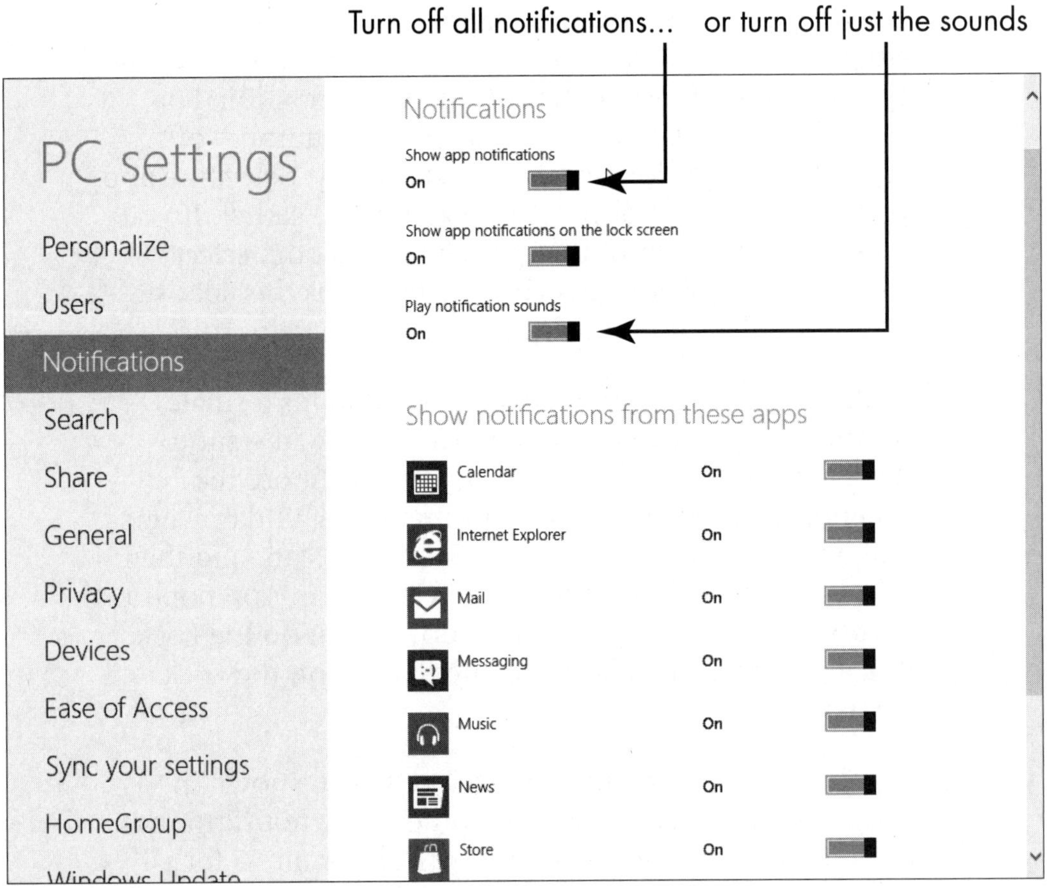

Turn off all notifications... or turn off just the sounds

Notifications

Show app notifications
On

Show app notifications on the lock screen
On

Play notification sounds
On

PC settings

Personalize

Users

Notifications

Search

Share

General

Privacy

Devices

Ease of Access

Sync your settings

HomeGroup

Windows Update

Show notifications from these apps

Calendar	On		
Internet Explorer	On		
Mail	On		
Messaging	On		
Music	On		
News	On		
Store	On		

Figure 8-14

Part III

Having Fun with Windows 8

The 5th Wave   By Rich Tennant

Don't get your hopes up, Ted. The other end may not be plugged in.

Installing Apps from the Microsoft Store

You can do many things with Windows 8, such as sending e-mail, browsing the Web, playing games, and looking at photos and videos. You can read the news and chat with family and friends. All these functions and more involve computer programs. Back in the day, such programs were called *applications*. Now, we call them *apps*.

Windows 8 comes with a few apps installed, such as the Weather and Travel apps. (See Chapter 2 for information on using these two apps and apps in general.) To obtain other apps — free or otherwise — you use the Microsoft Store.

To install an app from the Microsoft Store, you need a Microsoft Account. See Chapter 4 for information on setting up a Microsoft Account.

Microsoft tests and approves all apps in the Microsoft Store. For quality and security reasons, you can install Windows 8 apps only from the Microsoft Store.

In this chapter, you peruse the apps in the Microsoft Store, including those already installed on a new machine. You update existing apps, install a new one, and find out how to uninstall an app. Finally, you set up a payment method in case you want to buy an app.

Stroll through the Microsoft Store

1. On the Start menu, select the Store tile, which looks like a shopping bag with handles and the Windows logo, as shown in **Figure 9-1**.

Figure 9-1

2. Look over the Store home screen (see **Figure 9-2**). The Store is organized into categories that stretch off the right side of your screen, so scroll the screen right to see more.

Microsoft Store home screen

Figure 9-2

 To scroll with a mouse, roll the wheel or click the bottom of the screen. To scroll on a touchscreen, tap and then drag your finger from right to left or left to right. To use the keyboard to scroll, press the Page Down or Page Up keys. You can also use the Tab key to jump between sections or the right and left arrow keys to move through the screen one item at a time.

 Zoom out to see more categories by using one of the following methods: Press Ctrl as you roll the mouse wheel toward you, touch two fingers to the screen and move them together (pinch), or press Ctrl+- (the Ctrl key and the minus key).

3. Note the following category headings:

- **Spotlight:** View apps promoted from any category.

- **Games:** Play card games, solve puzzles and word games, and more.

- **Social:** Connect to friends and family.

- **Entertainment:** Check out apps that don't fit the other categories, such as those for drawing.

- **Photo:** View, edit, and share photos.

- **Music & Video:** Listen to music and watch movies.

- **Sports:** Follow your favorite sport or team. (Yeah, cricket!)

- **Books & Reference:** Read and research.

- **News & Weather:** Keep current.

- **Health & Fitness:** Want to get in shape? There's an app for that.

- **Food & Dining:** Locate eateries, as well as rate and review restaurants.

- **Lifestyle**: If you think entertainment is a vaguely defined category, check out lifestyle.

- **Shopping:** Put the world's catalogues at your fingertips.

- **Travel:** Get you there and back.

- **Finance:** Manage the money you don't spend on other apps.

- **Productivity:** Send e-mail and create schedules.

- **Tools:** Manage your computer.

- **Security:** Keep your computer and data safe.

- **Business:** Analyze business data.

- **Education:** Study the stars, languages, or piano, or prep for the SAT.

You may see other categories, as well.

 Is the app you want a game or entertainment? Will it make you productive or is it a tool? The category to which an app is assigned is determined by the app developer. In some cases, it's not clear why an app is in one category and not another. So it goes.

4. As you scroll the Store, you may see the following tiles within some of the categories:

- **Top Free** apps have the highest average rating among free apps in that category.

- **Top Paid** apps have the highest average rating among paid apps in that category.

- **All Stars** apps in the Spotlight category have the highest average rating from all categories.

- **New Releases** include apps recently added to the Store.

5. To return to the Store home screen from any other store screen, use one of the following methods:

- **Mouse:** With the mouse pointer in an empty area, click the right mouse button to display the app bar. Click Home.

- **Touchscreen**: Swipe down from the top or up from the bottom to display the app bar. Tap Home.

- **Keyboard**: Press ⊞+Z. Press the Enter key or the spacebar.

 The back arrow in the upper left of most screens takes you back one screen. The more screens you've stepped through, the more efficient it is to use the Home option on the app bar.

Explore Available Apps by Category

1. On the Start screen, select the Store app.

2. On the Store home screen, select the Games heading. The Games page appears, as shown in **Figure 9-3**, displaying tiles for various games.

3. Select All Subcategories and choose the Puzzle subcategory to display just puzzles.

 As you make selections in Steps 3–5, the apps matching selections appear automatically.

4. Select All Prices and then choose Free. (Trial apps are free for a trial period or a number of uses before you have to pay before continuing to use them.)

5. Select the Sort By drop-down box and then choose Sort by Highest Rating. The screen shown in **Figure 9-4** appears.

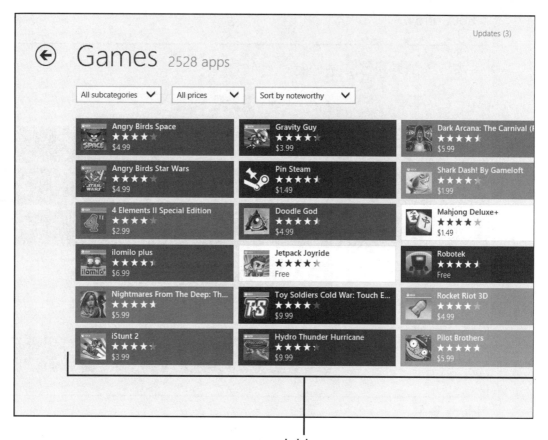

Available apps

Figure 9-3

 Use these steps to explore any app category.

6. Select the Mahjong Deluxe Free tile.

 If you don't see the Mahjong Deluxe Free tile, go to the next section, "Search for an App by Name."

7. Proceed to the "Install a New App" section, or return to the Store home screen.

Back arrow

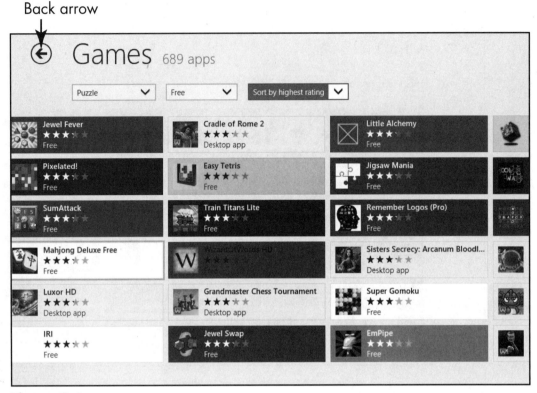

Figure 9-4

Search for an App by Name

1. On any Store screen, display the charms bar and then display the search panel using one of these methods:

- **Mouse:** Move the mouse pointer to the upper-left corner of the screen to display the charms bar. Then move the pointer down and click the Search charm.

- **Touchscreen:** Swipe from the right edge to display the charms bar. Tap Search.

- **Keyboard:** Press ⊞+Q (Q for *query*) to go directly to the search panel.

On the Store home screen, just start typing — no need to select Search first.

2. In the search box, type *mahjong*. As you type, potential matches appear below the search box, as shown in **Figure 9-5.** If you see Mahjong Deluxe Free, select it in the Search panel. (Don't select the paid version at this time.)

Figure 9-5

3. If you don't see Mahjong Deluxe below the search box, press the Enter key to search further. Select the app from the Results screen, as shown in **Figure 9-6.**

4. Proceed to the next section, "Install a New App," or return to the Store home screen.

Type search text here

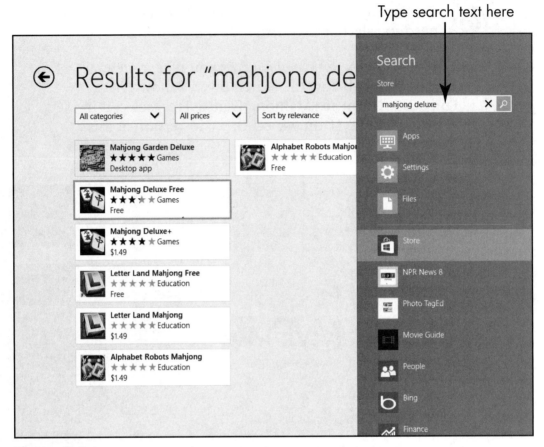

Figure 9-6

Install a New App

1. In the Store, display the Mahjong Deluxe Free screen. (See the section "Search for an App by Name" for details.)

2. The screen shown in **Figure 9-7** appears. This (and any) app screen has lots of information. Let's start at the top:

- The back arrow (left-pointing arrow in a circle) next to the Solitaire heading takes you back to the previously viewed screen. In this case, the back arrow takes you to your preinstalled apps.

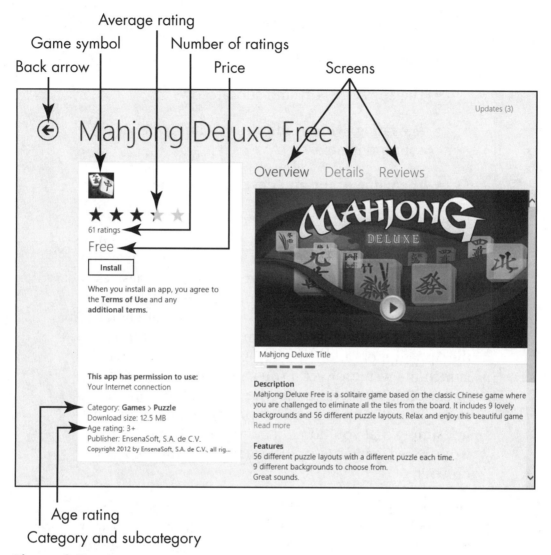

Figure 9-7

3. On the left side of the screen, note the following:

- The game symbol or icon, which also appears on the app tile

- The average rating in stars (5 stars is the best) and the number of times the app has been rated

- The cost of the app

- The cost of the app

- The Install button (don't click it just yet)

- The Terms of Use link

- The app's category and subcategory

- Age rating, which indicates suitability or age appropriateness

- The name of the app developer and the copyright

4. Looking to the right, note three options: Overview, Details, and Reviews. By default, the Overview screen displays a large preview of the app. Below the preview, the Description appears. The Features section emphasizes important aspects of the app. For example, Mahjong Deluxe Free boasts a large number of different layouts. At the bottom of the screen (you may have to scroll down), the App Support and Report App to Microsoft links launch the web browser. (You can report the app to Microsoft if you believe that the app is inappropriate due to content or purpose, such as promoting hate speech — not simply that you don't like the game or it doesn't work.) See Chapter 6 for information on the web browser.

 If the app has more than one preview, you'll see a > symbol to the right of the preview. Select the > symbol to move to the next preview, or select the < symbol (on the left) to move to the previous preview. The highlighting of the dashes below the preview subtly indicates which preview in the series of previews is on-screen currently.

5. For more technical information about the app, including its version number, select the Details option, at the top of the screen.

6. To view the reviews by users, first select the Reviews option, at the top of the screen. Then, next to Sort By, select the desired sort order.

> To read reviews that might help you determine whether you want to install a particular app, select Most Helpful.

7. Select the Install button (refer to **Figure 9-7**).

8. If you're not already signed in, enter your Microsoft Account e-mail address and password on the screen that pops up. Then select Sign In.

> Many apps are free. Before you buy an app, see the section "Add Billing Information to Microsoft Store."

> If you purchase an app, you are buying a license to install that app on up to five machines using the same Microsoft Account. The Microsoft Store will track how many times and on which machine the app is installed.

9. You return automatically to the screen you were on before Step 1. You may see *Installing Mahjong Deluxe Free* in the upper-right corner of the screen. When installation is complete, a brief notification appears on any screen you are viewing. You may also hear a beep.

> Installing an app may take a few seconds or a few minutes. You can do anything while an app installs — except use the app.

10. Display the Mahjong Deluxe Free screen again. In **Figure 9-8**, note that *You own this app* appears below the rating stars.

> If you don't see *You own this app*, the app may still be installing. If, after a few minutes, you still don't see this message, select the Install button again.

This message appears after the app is installed

Figure 9-8

11. To play Mahjong Deluxe Free or to use any app after you install it, return to the Start screen.

12. On the Start screen, the app you installed appears after all previously installed apps, as shown in **Figure 9-9**. Find the new tile for the app you installed (you may have to scroll right) and select that tile to open the app.

 To play Mahjong Deluxe Free, select the play button (the right-pointing triangle). Select Green Dragon to play. Choose the first game. Select uncovered tiles with matching symbols from any of the stacks on screen to remove pairs of tiles. Have fun!

New apps are on the far right

Figure 9-9

 You can move the Mahjong Deluxe tile on the Start screen. See Chapter 3 for information on rearranging tiles on the Start screen.

Examine Your Apps

1. To see which apps you have, display the app bar on any Store screen, using one of the following methods:

- **Mouse:** With the mouse pointer in an empty area, click the right mouse button.

- **Touchscreen:** Swipe down from the top or up from the bottom.

- **Keyboard:** Press ⊞+Z.

2. In the app bar that appears at the top of the screen, select Your Apps.

Use Home on the app bar to return to the Store home screen any time.

3. If you see a Sign In button, select that button and enter your Microsoft Account e-mail and password on the next screen.

4. On the screen shown in **Figure 9-10**, scroll to see which apps you have. Each tile displays an icon, the app name, and the purchase date (even for free apps). Lastly, each tile indicates *Installed* or *Not installed*.

How can you have an app you haven't installed? If you sign into more than one computer using your Microsoft Account, you might install an app on one machine but not another.

Most of these apps appear on your Start screen. For those that don't, you can find them by typing the app name on the Start screen.

5. Select the Apps Not Installed on this PC box. If you have signed in to more than one computer with your Microsoft Account, each computer is listed separately here, enabling you to see just those apps installed on a selected computer. (This option is irrelevant if you use only one computer.)

6. Select the Sort By box. As you install more apps, you may find it useful to Sort by Date (installed) or Sort by Name.

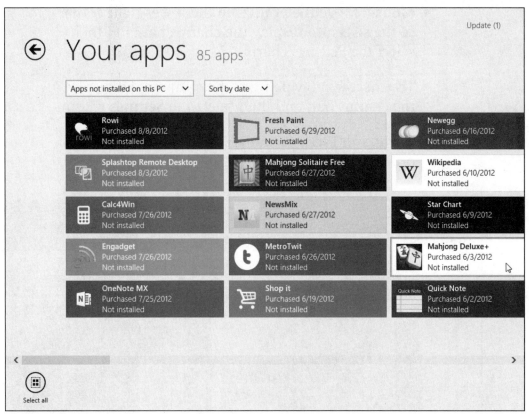

Figure 9-10

7. Select one of your installed apps. A check mark appears in the upper-right corner of the tile. Options appear at the bottom of the screen. You can install any app not yet installed on this computer. You can also view details for the selected app, as described in the preceding section.

8. Return to the Store home screen using the back arrow or the Home button on the app bar.

Update Installed Apps

1. To check for updates to your installed apps, display the settings options (shown in **Figure 9-11**) from any Store screen as follows:

- **Mouse:** Move the pointer to the lower-right corner of the screen to display the charms bar, and then select the Settings charm.

- **Touchscreen:** Swipe from the right side to display the charms bar, and then select the Settings charm.

- **Keyboard:** Press ⊞+I to go directly to the settings options.

Figure 9-11

 The Store tile on the Start screen displays the number of apps that have updates available, if any. If you don't see *Updates* in the upper right of any store screen, your apps are all up-to-date.

2. In the Settings panel, select App Updates.

3. On the App Updates screen, note that updates are automatically downloaded. This saves time when you decide to install updates. Select Check for Updates.

4. On the next screen, if you see *No updates available*, you're done. Return to the Store home screen.

5. When an app has an update available, the app tile is automatically selected, as indicated by the check mark. If you don't want a particular app updated at this time, select its tile to remove the check mark. If you decide to update the app later, simply select the tile again to add the check mark.

 Installing all available updates at once is easier than picking and choosing apps to update.

6. Select the Install button. You return automatically to the Store home screen (or whichever screen you were on when you selected the Updates option). The installation process happens quickly, so you may not see the *Installing updates* message in the upper-right corner.

 Updates install *in the background*, meaning you can do anything, including leaving the Store app, during the installation.

Rate and Review an App

1. On the Start screen, select the Mahjong Deluxe app. If you don't have this app, see the section "Install a New App" or substitute any app you have installed.

2. Display the Settings panel for the app you have on-screen. Select Rate and Review.

Every app has a Rate and Review option under Settings. You can also select Write a Review on the details screen for that app in the Microsoft Store.

You can rate or review only apps you've installed, and you must be signed in with your Microsoft Account. To rate or review a preinstalled app, install the app to associate the app with your Microsoft Account.

3. The Write a Review screen appears, as shown in **Figure 9-12**. Select the number of stars you want to give this app. (Select the first star on the left for the lowest rating up to the last star on the right for the highest rating.)

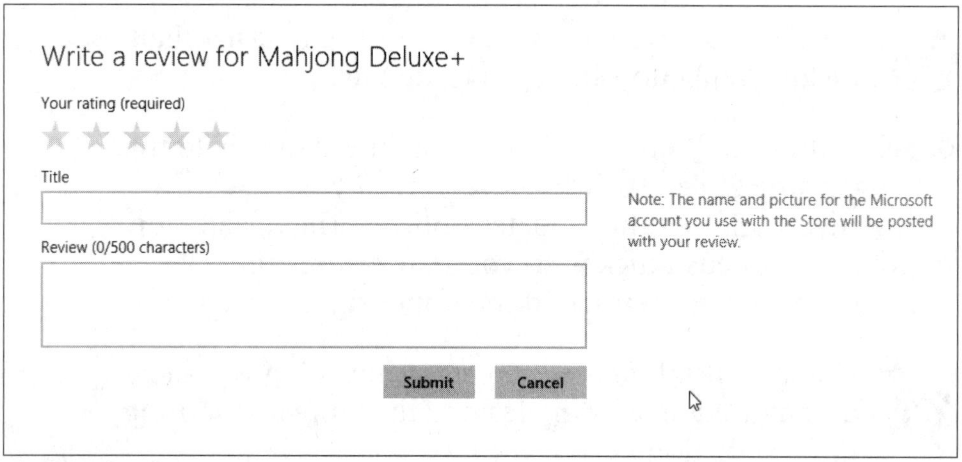

Write a review for Mahjong Deluxe+

Your rating (required)

★ ★ ★ ★ ★

Title

[   ]

Note: The name and picture for the Microsoft account you use with the Store will be posted with your review.

Review (0/500 characters)

[   ]

[Submit]   [Cancel]

Figure 9-12

If you want to rate the app but not review it, select Cancel. Select the star rating on the app screen (refer to **Figure 9-8**).

4. In the Title box, type a summary or overview of your comments, such as **Great app** or **Needs work**.

5. In the Review box, say what you will, up to 500 characters, including spaces and punctuation. Be helpful, if possible. Choose the Submit button when you're done with your review (or Cancel to abandon your review). The screen displays *Thank you. Your review will be posted soon.*

 Your comments may help another person decide whether or not to install an app. In addition, the app's developer may use customer feedback to fix problems or add features.

 Your Microsoft Account name and picture — but not your e-mail address — appear with your review.

6. On the app screen in Store, the option Update Your Review replaces Write a Review and your rating appears instead of the average rating. Your review will appear on the Reviews screen after some delay. You can update a review later, if your rating or comments change, but you can't retract or delete a review.

Uninstall an App

1. On the Start screen, locate Mahjong Deluxe or another app you want to remove from your computer. Use one of the following methods to select the app to uninstall:

- **Mouse:** Place the pointer over the app tile, and right-click (click the right mouse button) to display the app bar. Then click the Uninstall button.

- **Touchscreen:** Swipe down or up slightly on the app tile to select it without opening or moving it. The app bar is displayed. Tap the Uninstall button.

- **Keyboard:** Press the arrow keys to highlight the app, and then press the spacebar to select the app without opening it. Press ⊞+Z to display the app bar, use the arrow keys to highlight Uninstall, and then press the spacebar to begin the process.

2. A message appears to tell you that the app will be removed from your PC, as shown in **Figure 9-13**. (To cancel, click or tap anywhere outside the box.) To delete the app, select the Uninstall button. If you change your mind later, you can reinstall the app from the Store.

Uninstall the selected app

Figure 9-13

If you want to keep the app installed but remove its tile from the Start screen to reduce clutter, select Unpin from Start on the Start screen app bar. To find the app, use the search panel or find it in All Apps.

Add Billing Information to Microsoft Store

1. To add the billing information necessary to buy apps, select the Store tile on the Start screen. In the Store, display the Settings panel using one of these methods:

- **Mouse**: Move the mouse pointer into the lower-right corner to display the Charms bar. Click the Settings charm.

- **Touchscreen**: Swipe from the right edge. Tap the Settings charm.

- **Keyboard**: Press ⊞+I to go directly to the Settings panel.

2. In the Settings panel, select Your Account.

3. If you see Sign in to Windows Store, select the Sign In button. On the next screen, enter the e-mail address and password associated with your Microsoft Account. See Chapter 4 for information on creating a Microsoft Account.

4. On the Your Account screen, note the e-mail address. If this is not the account to which you want to add payment information, select Change User or Sign Out and enter the correct e-mail address and password.

5. Select Add Payment Method. The Payment and Billing screen appears, as shown in **Figure 9-14**.

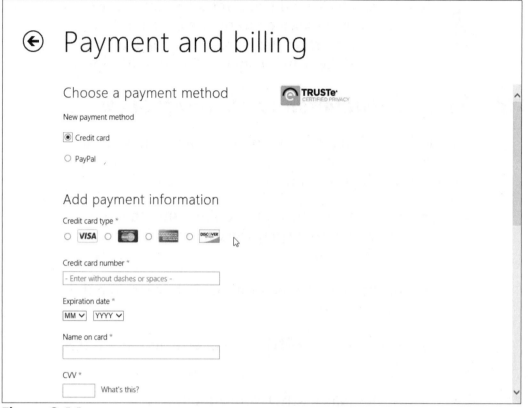

Figure 9-14

6. Under Choose a Payment Method, select Credit Card.

🎯 PayPal is a payment service. See www.paypal.com for information on creating a PayPal account. If you have a PayPal account, see the book's website (www.win8mjh.com) for information on using a PayPal account with the Microsoft Store.

7. In the Add Payment Information section, do the following:

- Select your credit card type.

🎯 All parts of this form require data except for Address Line 2.

- Enter your credit card number in the box provided. Don't enter dashes or spaces.

- Under Expiration Date, select the month (MM) and year (YYYY) your card expires.

- Enter your name as it appears on your credit card.

- Under CVV, enter the three- or four-digit verification code from your credit card. (Select What's This? for an illustration of the location of this code on your card.)

8. In the Billing Address section, do the following:

- Enter your street address, city, state, and zip code.

- Select your Country/region.

- Under Phone Number, enter your area code in the first box and the remainder of your number in the second box.

9. When you are ready to continue, select Submit.

10. If any of your data is incomplete or invalid, the form remains on screen. Look for indications of a problem. Review each entry before selecting Submit.

11. If your information was accepted, you return to the Your Account screen. Under Payment and billing info, note your credit card type, the last four digits of your number, and the expiration date.

12. To change, add, or view your credit card information, select Edit Payment Method. On the Payment and Billing screen, you can edit card information (except for type and number). You can also choose a new payment method.

Use the View Billing History link to open billing information in the web browser.

 For added security, select Yes under Always Ask for Your Password When Buying an App.

 Your payment and billing information is associated with your Microsoft Account. Any machine you sign in to using your Microsoft Account can be used to make purchases.

13. Select the back arrow to return to the Store. You can select Buy on any app information screen. See the section "Install a New App."

Taking Photos and More

Windows 8 makes enjoying digital photos
easy. You can pick and choose photos to
look at or display a group of photos in a slide
show. Make a favorite photo your Lock screen
background so you see it every time you start
Windows 8. In this chapter, you do all these
things.

Use the Paint app to crop a photo to remove
unwanted parts of the photo and draw
attention to the subject.

If you have a printer, you can print photos for
yourself or to send to someone. Even black-
and-white prints of color photos may be nice.

Of course, if you want to take your own
photos, nothing beats having a digital camera.
Copy photos from your camera to your
Pictures library for viewing and sharing. Or use
the Camera app with the built-in camera found
in many laptops and tablets.

In this chapter, you use the tools that come with Windows 8 for working with photos. You may want the additional features of a digital photo organizer and editing program. You might want to check out my book *Digital Photography For Seniors For Dummies* (Wiley) for detailed steps on organizing, editing, printing, and sharing photos as well as on using a digital camera.

 Check the book website at www.win8mjh.com for the latest information on ways to enjoy your photos.

Take Photos with Your Computer

1. Select the Camera app on the Start screen. If you don't have a webcam, the app screen displays *Connect a camera.* If you don't have a built-in webcam or the resolution of the one you have is too low, you can easily add a webcam. Simply plug the camera into your computer — it's that easy.

 You can choose from many good webcam models. Generally, get the highest video resolution you can afford, because you'll probably use the camera for video chats. Consider the size of the camera, its attachment to your computer, and whether or not it has a microphone (you want a mic).

2. The first time you use the Camera app, the screen displays *Can Camera use your webcam and microphone?* Select Allow to continue. (If you don't want to continue, don't choose Block unless you never expect to use this app. Instead, simply switch back to Start.)

3. The Camera app opens, and there's a good chance you recognize the face staring back at you. At least, I know the guy in **Figure 10-1.** To take a photo, smile and then click or tap anywhere on the image. You may hear a shutter click. Your photo is placed automatically in a folder called Camera Roll in the Pictures library.

Click or tap anywhere to take a photo

Figure 10-1

4. If you see Change Camera in the app bar, select that
option. Many tablets and laptops have two cameras, one
that faces you and one that points in the opposite direction. Switch to the camera away from you when you
want to use your computer for something other than a
self portrait. Take another picture — they're free. Select
Change Camera again to switch back to see yourself.

5. In the app bar, select Camera Options (refer to
Figure 10-1). You may see the following options:

- **Photo Resolution:** Higher resolution results in
  sharper images and larger files (in terms of
  required storage space, as well as width and

height). Generally, you want the highest resolution possible. The ratio in parentheses affects how completely the photo will fill a screen or a print. Traditionally, 4:3 was used for both screens and printing, but that has been changing. Odds are that your screen is 16:9, so this ratio may be best for you. Most prints are still 4:3, so you may want that ratio if you know you're going to print the photo. Experiment — you'll see the effect on-screen immediately.

- **Audio Device:** Relevant to video rather than photos, this option is limited to your built-in microphone unless you have more than one.

- **Video Stabilization:** Stability is good, especially for handheld video. Turn this on.

- **More:** Choose More to see sliders for Brightness and Contrast. Adjust these for the best exposure. Flicker applies to video and generally should be 60 Hz or higher.

6. Select Timer. Nothing happens until you click or tap the screen, at which point a countdown timer appears, giving you three seconds to compose yourself. Select Timer again to turn off this feature.

7. Select Video Mode. Nothing happens until you click or tap the screen, at which point you're in moving pictures. A counter indicates the length of the video. Short is sweet in video. You can speak, too. Click or tap the screen to stop the video. Your videos are in the Camera Roll folder in the Pictures library. Select Video Mode again to turn off this function and return to taking still photos (with the next click or tap).

8. Return to the Start screen. See the section "View Photos" to see the photos you just took.

Copy Photos from Your Camera

1. If your camera came with a cable, connect that cable to the camera, and then connect the other end of the cable to a USB port on your computer. If your laptop or tablet has a built-in card slot, you can take the memory card out of the camera and insert it in that slot.

 If your computer doesn't have a built-in card slot, consider buying a small memory card reader that plugs into your computer and works with your camera's memory card. You don't need a multicard reader, just a reader with a single slot the size of your camera card. I consider a card reader more convenient than using a cable.

2. Windows 8 detects your camera or its memory card and may briefly display a notification indicating *Tap to choose what happens with memory cards.* (You can also click the notification.) If you're quick enough to tap or click the first notification, Windows 8 displays your choices, as shown in **Figure 10-2**. Select Import Photos and Videos, if that option is available, and then skip to Step 4. If you don't catch the notification in time, continue to Step 3 to import photos another way.

 See Chapter 3 for information on increasing the time a notification remains on-screen.

3. Start the Photos app, and then display the app bar by right-clicking, by swiping down or up, or by pressing ▦ +Z. Select the Import button. No need for lightning reflexes. If you see more than one removable disk listed, your card is probably *D:*. If you choose the wrong disk, you'll recognize that fact in the next step, and you can repeat this step with a different disk.

Select the Photos app

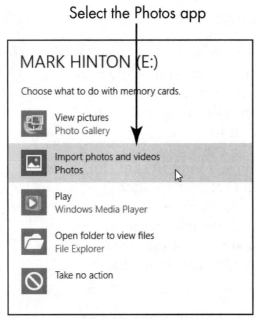

Figure 10-2

4. Your photos appear on the Removable Disk screen, as shown in **Figure 10-3**. All photos are selected and ready to be imported to your Pictures library. In most cases, you'll import all photos. If you don't want all photos, select the ones you don't want, to remove their check mark. Or choose Clear Selection and select the photos you do want to import. Note the indication near the bottom of the screen that these photos will be put in a folder with a name based on today's date. You may want to change that name to something more meaningful, such as **Vacation** or **Flowers**. You can clear the text from that box to put the photos directly in the Pictures library instead of in a folder in the library. When you're ready, select the Import button.

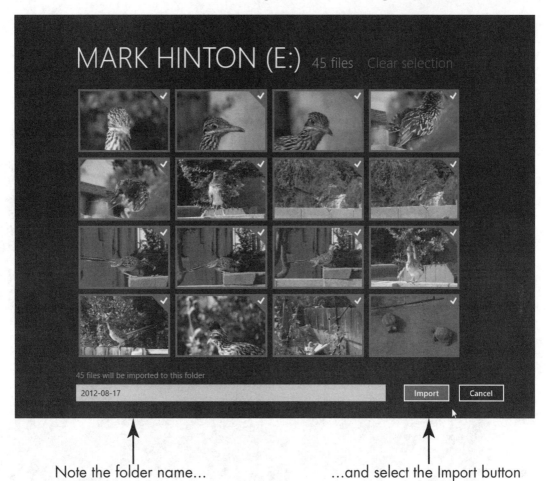

Note the folder name...   ...and select the Import button

Figure 10-3

Organizing photos can be a challenge. If you dump more than a few dozen photos into the Pictures library without using folders, finding a specific photo later will be difficult. Using folders with unintelligible names doesn't help, either. Most of my folder names are based on the year and month (such as 2012-06) or the subject, such as Luke the Lovehound.

5. A progress bar flashes as your photos are imported. When the process is complete, the screen displays *Done!* and indicates how many photos were imported and into which folder, if any. For example, **Figure 10-4** shows that I imported three files into a folder called 2012-06. Select Open Folder, and then scroll through your photos.

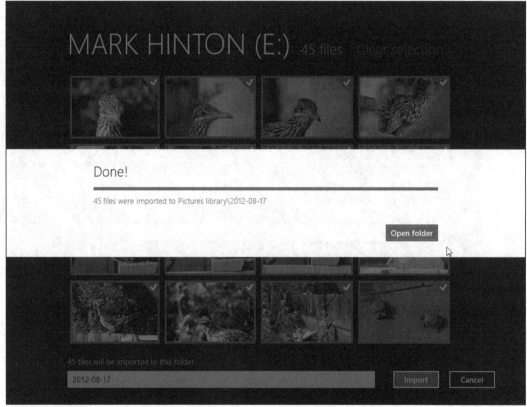

MARK HINTON (E:) 45 files   Clear selection

Done!

45 files were imported to Pictures library\2012-08-17

Open folder

45 files will be imported to this folder

2012-08-17   Import   Cancel

Figure 10-4

If the photos on your memory card don't import automatically the next time you copy photos, you can tell Windows 8 how to handle memory cards. On the Start screen, type **autoplay**. In the Search panel, select Settings. In the Results screen, select AutoPlay. The AutoPlay control panel window opens on the desktop. In the Camera Storage section, select the box next to Memory Card. Select Import Photos and Videos (Photos) from the available options and then select Save. Switch back to the Start screen. Remove your memory card or disconnect the camera cable. Reinsert or reconnect. This method for changing AutoPlay may be helpful for other media types or devices.

View Photos

1. To see photos on your computer, select the Photos app on the Start screen. The Photos home screen opens, as shown in **Figure 10-5.** Your screen will look different. Scroll to the right, noting the following photo categories:

- **Pictures Library:** Photos on your computer are in your Pictures library. You'll see Add Some Photos if there aren't any in your library.

- **SkyDrive Photos:** These photos are in the cloud, which means stored remotely on a Microsoft website and accessible on any machine you sign in to with your Microsoft Account.

- **Facebook Photos:** If you have signed in to your Facebook account, your Facebook photos are here. Otherwise, the tile displays *See yours here.* Some other time, select this tile to sign in to your Facebook account.

- **Flickr Photos:** Flickr is a very popular website for sharing photos. If you have signed in to your Flickr account, you can access your photos through this category. Otherwise, the tile displays *See yours here.* Some other time, select this tile to sign in to your Flickr account.

- **Devices:** If you sign in to more than one computer using the same Microsoft Account, use Devices to access photos stored on a different computer.

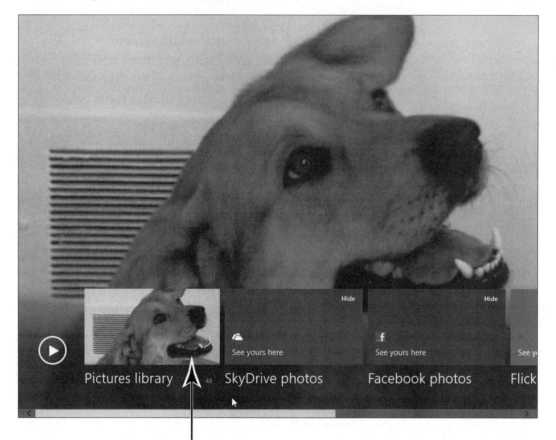

Your Pictures library

Figure 10-5

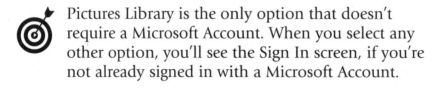 Pictures Library is the only option that doesn't require a Microsoft Account. When you select any other option, you'll see the Sign In screen, if you're not already signed in with a Microsoft Account.

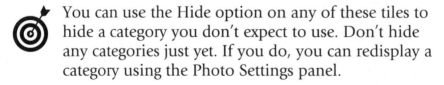 You can use the Hide option on any of these tiles to hide a category you don't expect to use. Don't hide any categories just yet. If you do, you can redisplay a category using the Photo Settings panel.

2. Select the Pictures Library. If you don't see any pictures, skip to one of the following sections:

- If you have a digital camera, see "Copy Photos from Your Camera."

- If your computer has a built-in camera or a webcam, see "Take Photos with Your Computer."

3. If you see pictures in your Pictures Library, scroll to the right to see more photos.

 You can take a screenshot — a picture of the current screen — by pressing ⊞+Print Screen. (A touchscreen or mouse equivalent is not available.) The screen dims slightly to indicate the capture, which is stored automatically in the Screenshots folder in your Pictures library. Use this technique to create your own documentation of problems or something you want to see again later.

4. If necessary, select a folder in your Pictures library (folders appear first, followed by photos). Scroll to the right through your photos. Select any photo to see it full screen. (Due to proportions, the photo may fill only the width or the height, not both.) Scroll through the full-screen photos by clicking or tapping the right edge of the screen (to go forward) or the left edge (to go back). Press the PageDown key (forward) or PageUp key (back).

5. Display the app bar, as shown in **Figure 10-6**. Select the Slide Show button. The photos in your album appear full screen in succession. (If you don't want to wait, click or tap the photo to change to the next.) Stop the slide show by selecting a photo or by displaying the app bar again. Use the back arrow to return to the folder.

 On the Photos home page (refer to **Figure 10-5**), select the triangle to the left of the Pictures Library for a different kind of slideshow, in which multiple photos are tiled in a mosaic.

Figure 10-6

6. Zoom in and out on a photo using one of these methods (repeat to zoom in or out more):

- **Mouse:** Click the plus sign in the lower-right corner to zoom in. (Ignore the charms bar, if it appears.) Click the minus sign to zoom out.

- **Touchscreen:** Touch two fingers on the screen. Move your fingers apart to zoom in. Pinch your fingers closer together to zoom out.

- **Keyboard:** Press Ctrl+plus sign (actually, press the equals sign — no need to press the Shift key) to zoom in. Press Ctrl+minus sign to zoom out.

 Zoom in for to see part of a photo made larger. Zoom out as far as you can to see many photos at once.

7. Select one of your photos to display it full screen. Display the app bar. Select the Set As button and note the following options, using any or all if you want:

- **Lock Screen:** Set one of your own photos as the one that appears on the Lock screen.

- **App Tile:** By default, the Photo app tile displays photos from your Pictures library, unless the Live Tile option is off. If you prefer, you can set a single photo as the one on the Photo app tile.

- **App Background:** This photo is the one on the Photos home screen (refer to **Figure 10-5**).

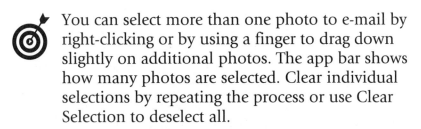 Use the Delete button in the app bar to delete all photos you selected using a right mouse click or a tap and drag. Note the number of selected photos to the left of the Delete button. Be certain you don't have more photos selected than you realize. See Chapter 14 for information on undeleting files.

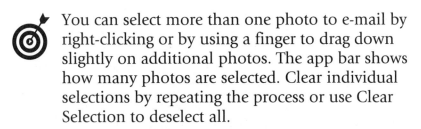 As this book goes to press, the Photos app does not have any options for editing photos. I recommend Windows Photo Gallery. See Chapter 12 for information on installing Photo Gallery. Check the book's website (www.win8mjh.com) for the latest on editing photos. See the section "Edit Photos Using Paint."

Share Photos by E-Mail

1. In the Photos app, select one of your photos.

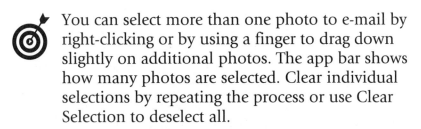 You can select more than one photo to e-mail by right-clicking or by using a finger to drag down slightly on additional photos. The app bar shows how many photos are selected. Clear individual selections by repeating the process or use Clear Selection to deselect all.

2. Display the Share panel using one of the following methods:

- **Mouse:** Move the mouse pointer to the upper-right corner of the screen. On the charms bar, select the Share charm.

- **Touchscreen:** Swipe from the right edge of the screen. Tap the Share charm.

- **Keyboard:** Press ■+H (think *sHare*) to go straight to the Share panel.

3. On the Share panel, select the Mail tile. (The number of selected photos appears in the Share panel.)

 You can share using any apps that appear in the Share panel.

4. The Mail panel slides in from the right, as shown in **Figure 10-7.** Enter an e-mail address under To. Add a subject. A thumbnail image of the selected image appears in the content area. You can add a message below the photo. When you're ready, select the Send button in the upper-right corner. The Mail panel indicates *Sending email.*

 The next time you use the Share panel in Internet Explorer or another app that shares with Mail, the e-mail address you used in Step 4 appears near the top of the panel. Select that address to save time when sharing something else with that person.

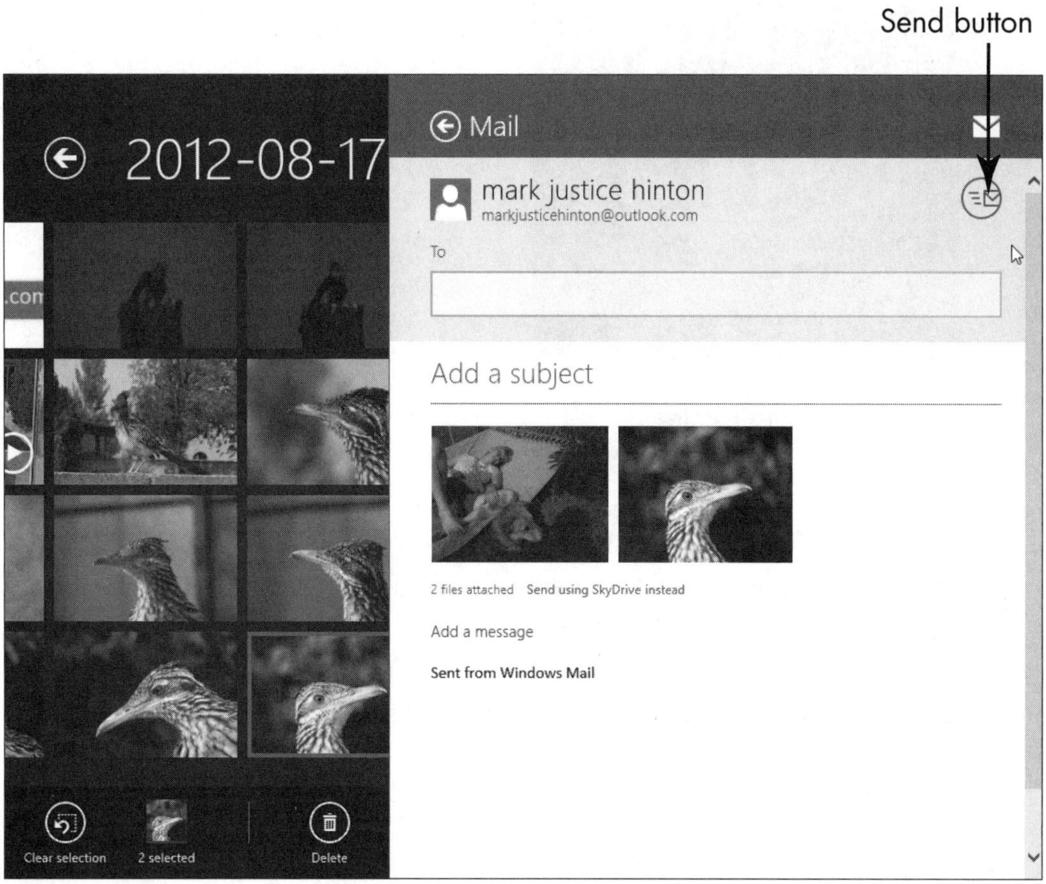

Send button

Figure 10-7

Print Photos Using the Photo App

1. In the Photo app, select one photo using a click or tap for full-screen viewing.

2. Display the charms bar, and then select Devices. A list of printers appears, as shown in **Figure 10-8.** Select your printer.

Select your printer

Figure 10-8

 If you have a printer but it doesn't appear in the list, you may not have selected a photo or you may have two or more photos selected. As this book goes to press, the Photos app doesn't have an option for printing more than one photo at a time. Check the book's website (www.win8mjh.com) for updates on printing photos.

3. The Printer panel expands into view, as shown in **Figure 10-9.** Note the preview. Select the Print button. (To cancel, use the back arrow or select anywhere outside the Printer panel.)

 Here's a handy keyboard shortcut that works in any app: Press ⊞+K to display the Devices panel. The shortcut Ctrl+P opens the Printer panel directly in some apps, but not all.

Check the preview

Figure 10-9

Edit Photos Using Paint

1. You can use the Paint accessory to make changes to a photo, including making a picture smaller. On the Start screen, type **paint**. In the Apps search results, select Paint, which opens on the desktop. See Chapter 5 for information on using the desktop.

2. In the ribbon at the top of Paint, select the File tab, and then select Open. The Open window displays photos in your Pictures library. If necessary, double-click or double-tap a folder to locate the photo with which you want to work. Select the photo and then select Open.

3. Because Paint opens photos full-sized, you see only a portion of the photo. In the lower-right corner of the Paint window, select the Zoom Out (minus sign) button or drag the slider to the left. The photo in **Figure 10-10** is shown at 12.5% magnification. Zoom in and out as necessary to work with different areas of the photo.

Zoom to see it all

Figure 10-10

4. Before you make any changes to this photo, consider saving a copy so you can retain the original. Making duplicates gives you some insurance against edits you can't undo, but you may not want to duplicate every photo. Select the File tab, and then select Save As. You can ignore the menu of file types that pops out to the side.

5. Change the name in the File Name box to create a new copy of this picture — you might want to just add 2. Select Save. You're now editing the copy; the original file exists under the original name and will remain unaltered.

6. Many photos can be improved by *cropping,* which involves cutting out distracting elements and keeping just part of the photo. You might crop a photo to concentrate on its most important part. To crop, click or tap Select in the Image section of the ribbon. In the photo, click (or tap) and drag a box over the area you want to keep — everything outside this box will be deleted. With practice, you can change the area selected by dragging the tiny square handles that appear in each corner and in the middle of each side.

Selecting the right area can be awkward. To start over, click or tap Select again.

7. Select Crop. The selected area is all that remains, as shown in **Figure 10-11**. If you crop a very small area, you may want to zoom in to see the results.

Crop tool

Figure 10-11

You can undo each step by selecting the Undo button above the Home tab (or by pressing Ctrl+Z).

8. If you want to save the changed photo, select the Save button.

 After you update the Photo app (see Chapter 9), you'll find a Crop tool in the app bar for a selected photo.

 Windows Photo Gallery is a great tool for viewing, organizing, editing, and printing photos. See the book's website (www.win8mjh.com) for a link to Photo Gallery, or search the Store for the latest photo apps. See Chapter 12 for information on installing Windows Photo Gallery.

Enjoying Music and Videos

*T*he term *media* on computers refers to something other than text: Audio and video are examples of media. *Audio* is a catchall term for music and other sound files, such as books on CD. *Video* includes files you can shoot with your digital camera, as well as Hollywood blockbusters.

The delivery of music has come a long way from Edison's wax cylinder or even vinyl LPs. Nowadays, music is entirely digital. The Music app lets you play your music collection and makes it easy to explore new music. Use Windows Media Player to play audio CDs and to copy audio files to your music library.

The Video app is similar to the Music app, but for video instead of music. You can use either app to buy new media, as well as play what you have.

In this chapter, you play a CD and copy CDs to the music library for easier access. You also explore the Music and Video apps.

You'll need a different app to play DVDs. Search Microsoft Store for Media Center or for a DVD player app. See Chapter 9 for more information on Microsoft Store.

 Popular alternatives for music or videos include Amazon, Hulu, Netflix, and YouTube. All these are accessible through the web browser. Search Microsoft Store for related apps.

Play and Copy Music from a CD

1. If you have a CD or DVD disc drive or slot on your computer, insert a music CD, label side up for horizontal drives. (Vertical drives are less predictable.)

2. Windows 8 detects your CD and may briefly display a notification indicating *Tap to choose what happens with audio CDs.* (You can also click the notification.) If you're quick enough to tap or click the first notification, Windows 8 displays your choices, as shown in **Figure 11-1.** Select Windows Media Player, and then skip to Step 5.

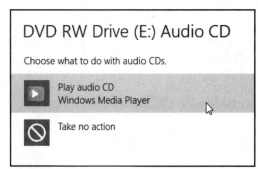

Figure 11-1

 If using the Music app is an option, see the book's website (www.win8mjh.com) for more information.

See Chapter 3 for information on increasing the time a notification remains on-screen.

3. If you missed the notification, select the Desktop tile on the Start screen. On the desktop, select the File Explorer icon (which looks like a folder) in the taskbar.

4. On the left side of File Explorer, select Computer, and then the drive below Local Disk C:. You may see the words *Audio CD*.

5. In the ribbon, select the Manage tab under Drive Tools. Then select AutoPlay. The notification from Step 1 reappears (and stays on-screen until you select something). Select Windows Media Player, unless the Music app is available, in which case select the Music app and skip to the next section.

6. If you see the Welcome to Windows Media Player screen, select Recommended Settings, and then select Finish. The Windows Media Player plays your music on the desktop. Switch back to the Start screen. The music continues to play. Switch back to the desktop.

7. For access to more options, select Switch to Library, a small button under the X in Windows Media Player, as shown in **Figure 11-2**.

Switch to Library

Figure 11-2

8. Note the following controls at the bottom of the Media Player, as shown in **Figure 11-3**:

- **Shuffle:** Select this button to turn on *shuffle,* which randomly mixes the tracks you play. Select again to turn off shuffle, and the tracks play in the order in which they appear on-screen.

- **Repeat:** Select this button to play all the tracks again after all have played. Select again to turn off the repeat function.

- **Stop:** Select to stop playing.

- **Previous:** Select this button to skip to the previous track. Select and hold to rewind to an earlier point in the track.

- **Play/Pause:** Select the button with two vertical lines to pause play mid-track. Select the same button (now with a triangle pointing to the right) to resume playing from the point you paused.

- **Next:** Select this button to skip to the next track. Select and hold to fast-forward through the track.

- **Mute/Unmute:** Select this button to silence the player. Although the track continues to play, you won't hear it. When mute is on, a red circle with a slash appears next to the speaker icon. Select the button again to hear the track.

- **Volume:** Drag the slider to the left to decrease or to the right to increase the volume of the track. Your speakers may also have a manual volume control. Windows 8 has a separate volume control in the taskbar, as well.

- **Now Playing:** Located far to the right of the toolbar, select this button to reduce the player to a small size (refer to **Figure 11-2**).

Control music playback

Switch to Now Playing

Figure 11-3

9. To copy the CD tracks to your Music library, select Rip CD.

> Be sure to refer to this as *ripping a CD* around your younger friends. But not the youngest, because they think CDs are way passé and MP3s rule. (MP3 is an audio file format common to portable digital music players and music downloads.)

> If you're going to rip a lot of CDs, select Rip Settings⇨Rip CD Automatically and Rip Settings⇨ Eject CD After Ripping. Just inserting the CD will copy files to your Music library as it plays the CD. Audiophiles should choose Rip Settings⇨Audio Quality⇨192 Kbps (Best Quality).

10. When the copying process finishes, remove your CD. To play this music in the future, start the Media Player and choose Artist, Album, or Genre under Music. You can also play anything in the Music library using the Music app. See the next section, "Listen to the Music App."

 Pin the Media Player to the taskbar for easy access: Click the right mouse button over the icon in the taskbar, or tap and hold until a box appears and then release. On the menu that pops up, select Pin This Program to Taskbar. You can also search for Windows Media Player on the Start screen. See Chapter 2 for information on pinning apps to the Start screen.

 If your music CD doesn't play automatically the next time you insert one, you can tell Windows 8 how to handle audio CDs. On the Start screen, type **auto-play**. In the Search panel, select Settings. In the Results screen, select AutoPlay. The AutoPlay control panel window opens on the desktop. Under CDs, select the box next to Audio CD. Select Windows Media Player from the available options, unless you see a different app you'd rather use, such as the Music app. Then select Save. Switch back to the Start screen. Remove your CD, and then reinsert it. This method for changing AutoPlay may be helpful for other media types or devices.

Listen to the Music App

1. Select the Music app on the Start screen. The Xbox Music app home screen appears.

2. Scroll to the right for an overview of the Xbox Music home screen. Scroll to the left, possibly past the first screen you saw, to see your music, labeled *my music*. If the Music library doesn't contain any music, you may see *It's lonely here* (which is not the title of a song). If you see music here, ignore it for the moment. (Or select your music and skip to Step 7, and do the rest of the steps some other time.) **Figure 11-4** shows the album I ripped from a CD in the preceding section.

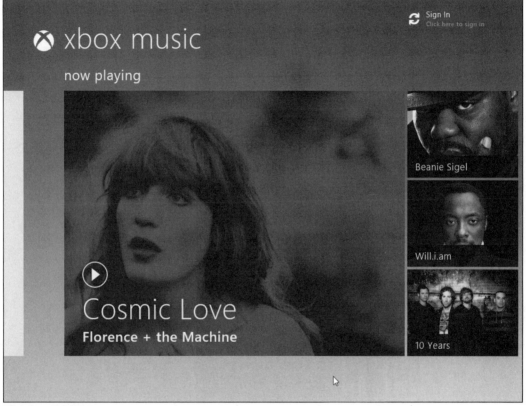

Figure 11-4

 If you see *Can't sign in*, you're not connected using a Microsoft Account. You'll still be able to do the steps in this section. You need to sign in only to buy music.

3. To search for music by title or artist, start the search function using one of the following methods:

- **Mouse:** Move the mouse pointer to the upper-right corner of the screen to display the charms bar. Select the Search charm.

- **Touchscreen:** Swipe from the right edge, and then tap Search.

- **Keyboard:** Press ⊞+Q (for *Query*) to go straight to Search.

4. In the Search panel, type the text for which you want to search. As you type, suggested matches appear below the text box. For now, ignore these suggestions (but take advantage of them in the future to save typing). Instead, select the magnifying glass or press Enter. Search results appear on the left. Select any search result for the next step.

 Selecting a suggested match may take you directly to Artist Details. Not a bad place to end up, but you can't easily get from there to the next step without repeating Step 4.

5. If the songs screen opened, as shown in **Figure 11-5**, note the following options (not all of which may appear on the current screen):

- **Open File:** You can browse your Music library using this control or from the My Music screen.

- **Buy:** You must sign in to continue. An option to buy also appears if you select an individual song.

- **Preview:** This option plays a sample of the selected music.

- **Play on Xbox:** This option plays the selection on an Xbox game console. (Selecting this option displays *Get xbox companion from the Store*, unless you've already installed that app.)

- **Details:** This option opens a biographical page with links to play all or show a list of related songs.

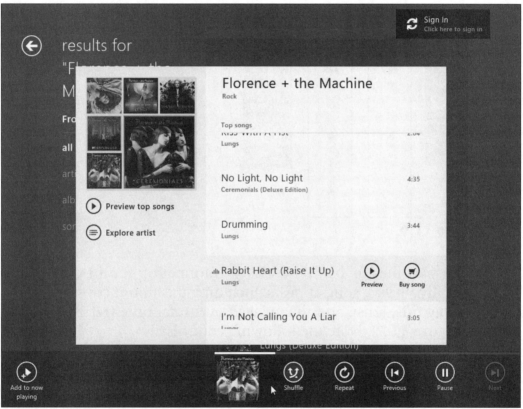

Figure 11-5

6. Select Preview Top Songs (or Preview), which plays short samples from the selected music.

7. Check the volume level on your speakers. Tablets and laptops often have physical volume controls — look around the edges. To adjust volume levels using Windows 8, display the Settings panel. Select the speaker icon above the Power control, as shown in **Figure 11-6**. Slide the control up for more volume and down for less. Select the speaker icon to mute or unmute all sounds. Speakers should be unmuted but not so loud as to cause bleeding. Select anywhere in the Songs area to dismiss the Settings panel.

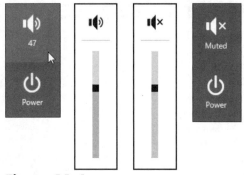

Figure 11-6

8. Display the app bar, if necessary. Information for the currently playing song appears, including the album cover, song title, artist, and time played over total time (refer to **Figure 11-5**). Note the following controls:

- **Add to Now Playing:** Select to build a playlist of multiple tunes.

- **Shuffle:** Select to play tracks randomly. Select again to play in the order listed on the screen.

- **Repeat:** Don't every stop.

- **Previous:** Go back one track.

- **Pause** or **Play:** Pause the track and the button changes to Play. Select Play to resume. There is no separate Stop button. You have to pause indefinitely or close the app.

- **Next:** Go forward one track.

 Your keyboard may have similar controls.

9. Switch back to the Start screen. The Music app continues to play. The Music tile displays the album art and title of the current song. Select the Music tile to return to the app.

 You may be able to play music from your computer to another device, such as another computer, a Windows Phone, an Xbox, or a TV on your network. Display the charms bar and select Devices to see if any are available.

10. Select anywhere outside the songs window to dismiss that window.

11. Although you don't have to close the app, if you want to close the Music app or any other, use one of the following methods:

- **Mouse:** Move the mouse pointer to the top of the window. Click and drag down, and then release the mouse button.

- **Touchscreen:** Swipe down from the top edge until the app window shrinks. Lift your finger.

- **Keyboard:** Press Alt+F4.

Watch Videos

1. Select the Video app on the Start screen. The Xbox Video app home screen appears. See **Figure 11-7.** Scroll to the right for an overview of the Video home screen, noting Movies Marketplace and TV Marketplace. Scroll to the left, possibly past the first screen you saw, to see your videos, labeled *my videos*. If the Video library does not contain any videos, you may see *It's lonely here.* If you see videos here, ignore those videos for the moment.

Figure 11-7

 If you see *Can't sign in*, you're not connected using a Microsoft Account. You'll be able to do the steps in this section. You need to be signed in only to buy or rent videos.

2. To search for videos by title or artist, start the search function with one of the following methods:

- **Mouse:** Move the mouse pointer to the upper-right corner of the screen to display the charms bar. Select the Search charm.

- **Touchscreen:** Swipe from the right edge, and then tap Search.

- **Keyboard:** Press ⊞+Q (for *Query*) to go straight to Search.

3. In the Search panel, type the text for which you want to search. As you type, suggested matches appear below the text box. For now, ignore these suggestions (but take advantage of them in the future to save typing). Instead, select the magnifying glass or press Enter. Search results appear on the left. Select any search result for the next step.

 Selecting a suggested match may take you directly to the Details screen. Not a bad place to end up, but you can't easily get from there to the next step without repeating Step 3.

4. If the description screen opened, as shown in **Figure 11-8**, note the following options (not all of which may appear on the current screen):

- **View Seasons:** For a TV series, see information on the individual seasons and episodes.

- **Rent:** You must sign in to continue.

- **Buy:** You must sign in to continue.

- **Explore:** This option opens a biographical page with an overview of the movie or TV series.

- **Play Trailer:** Play the preview for the selected movie.

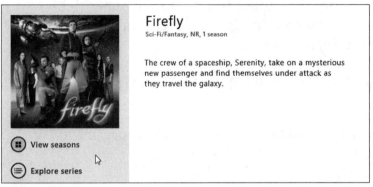

Figure 11-8

5. Select Play Trailer. (If you don't see that option, select a movie from the Video home screen or search for a movie.)

6. Check the volume level on your speakers. Tablets and laptops often have physical volume controls — look around the edges. To adjust volume levels using Windows 8, display the Settings panel. Select the speaker icon above the Power control (refer to **Figure 11-6**). Slide the control up for more volume and down for less volume. Select the speaker icon to mute or unmute all sounds. Speakers should be unmuted but not so loud as to cause bleeding. Select anywhere outside the Settings panel to dismiss it.

7. Display the app bar. Note the following controls, shown in **Figure 11-9**:

- **Open File:** You can browse your Video library using this control or from the My Videos screen.

- **Repeat:** Don't every stop.

- **Previous:** Go back.

- **Pause** or **Play:** Pause the video and the button changes to Play. Select Play to resume. There isn't a separate Stop button. You have to Pause indefinitely or close the app.

- **Next:** Go forward.

- **Play on Xbox:** This option plays the selection on an Xbox game console.

Figure 11-9

 Your keyboard may have similar controls.

8. Switch back to the Start screen. The Video app pauses automatically — no need to use the Pause control. The Video tile displays the title of the video currently paused.

Select the Video tile to return to the app, which automatically resumes playing.

 You may be able to play video from your computer to another device, such as another computer, a Windows Phone, an Xbox, or a TV on your network. Display the charms bar and select Devices to see if any are available.

9. Although you don't have to close the app, if you want to close the Video app or any other, use one of the following methods:

- **Mouse:** Move the mouse pointer to the top of the window. Click and drag down, and then release the mouse button.

- **Touchscreen:** Swipe down from the top edge until the app window shrinks, and then lift your finger.

- **Keyboard:** Press Alt+F4.

 Use the Camera app to record your own videos, which are saved automatically in the Camera Roll folder in the Pictures library. Then use the Open File control on the Video app bar to open the video. (You can also play back your camera videos in the Photos app.)

 For complete information on movies, TV, and the people involved in either, see www.imdb.com.

Part IV
Beyond the Basics

The 5th Wave   By Rich Tennant

"The funny thing is he's spent 9 hours organizing his computer desktop."

Maintaining Windows 8

*T*he desktop originated long before Windows 8. (In fact, desktops used to be made of wood.) Now, the desktop has changed into something more than just another app but less than the Windows centerpiece it once was.

Windows 8 uses the *Action Center* to keep you informed of security and maintenance issues that may need attention, such as antivirus protection. The Action Center divides issues into Security and Maintenance sections. The Reliability Monitor can help you pinpoint problems with hardware and software.

As millions of people put Windows 8 to the test every single hour, Microsoft discovers glitches with how Windows 8 works. Especially important are weaknesses in security that turn up only when software is under fire in the real world. *Windows Update* is the process for installing *patches* (updates) to plug these holes in Windows 8.

If you have an always-on Internet connection, such as DSL or cable, Windows Update automatically downloads and installs the most important updates as they become available (usually, once a month). Security patches are one of the most important updates, so they're among the updates installed automatically.

Chapter 12

Get ready to . . .

Optional updates include updates to device *drivers*, the programs that make Windows 8 work with specific hardware, such as your display and printer. Windows Update keeps track of optional updates but leaves the decision of whether to install — and the installation — up to you. For this reason, you need to run Windows Update on the desktop and check for optional updates every few months.

Machines such as toaster ovens aren't getting any smarter. Your computer, however, can be programmed to do something it's never done before. To make your computer capable of doing new things, you install new programs. On the other hand, your computer may have some programs that you'll never use and wouldn't miss. You don't have to get rid of them, but doing so is easy enough and frees a little space on your computer.

In this chapter, you work with the Action Center and Windows Update. You also install a program on the desktop and, optionally, uninstall one.

 Updates to Windows 8 apps are handled by the Windows Store app on the Start screen. See Chapter 9 for information on updating individual apps.

Explore System Information on the Desktop

1. On the Start screen, select the Desktop tile. On the desktop, display the Settings panel using one of these techniques:

- **Mouse:** Move the mouse pointer into the lower-right corner of the screen. Select the Settings charm from the charms bar.

- **Touchscreen:** Swipe from the right edge and tap Settings.

- **Keyboard:** Press ⊞+I.

2. In the Settings panel, select PC Info. The System window in **Figure 12-1** appears. This screen is chockfull of information and functions. Note each of the following areas on screen:

System information on the desktop

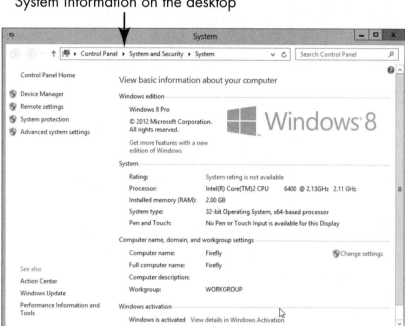

Figure 12-1

- **Windows edition:** Of course, you have Windows 8. However, Windows 8 comes in two primary editions: the standard edition, which you are likely to have, and the Pro edition, for computer professionals. You may find information here about so-called Service Packs, large collections of updates to Windows 8.

- **System:** This section displays details about your hardware, including the processor, the amount of installed memory (RAM), and other details. Values range from an anemic 1.0 to a smokin' 9.9. The displayed rating can be used to compare two machines. Generally, a higher rating is better, although you can delve deeper into the subject by selecting Windows Experience Index (some other time).

 The Windows Experience Index rates five components of your computer. The lowest score becomes the overall rating (not an average of separate scores). This rating can identify the weakest component in your computer, which you may be able to replace for improved performance. See the website `www.win8mjh.com` for more information.

- **Computer name, domain, and workgroup settings:** This information pertains to your network, if any. If a computer can't connect to a network, the problem is often related to the name of the Workgroup (a network). The Change Settings function lets you change the Workgroup name to match other computers on the same network. See Chapter 14 for information on networks, including workgroups and homegroups.

- **Windows activation:** In an effort to control software piracy involving bootlegged copies of Windows 8, each copy of Windows 8 must be activated. Odds are that you activated your copy the first time you started your computer. If you don't see *Windows is activated* in this section, select the adjacent link.

 Don't be alarmed by the System information and options. If all goes well, you don't have to use most of what you find here. Some familiarity with this screen will be useful, however, is all doesn't go well later.

Check the Action Center

1. In the System window (refer to **Figure 12-1**), select Action Center in the lower-left corner. The Action Center window appears, as shown in **Figure 12-2**.

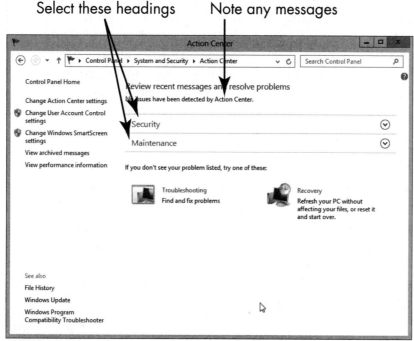

Figure 12-2

 Another way to open the Action Center is to search on the Start screen for **Action Center**, and then select the Settings category.

2. Note any message displayed under Review Recent Messages and Resolve Problems. Ideally, you see *No issues have been detected by Action Center*. If you see a message concerning a specific problem, select that message for more information.

3. Select the Security heading in the Action Center. That section expands to detail security functions. Every option but one should display *On* or *OK*. The exception is Network Access Protection, a function normally found in corporate environments. Here's a brief description of each item under Security:

- **Network Firewall:** The firewall scans Internet traffic and blocks activity from programs that don't have explicit permission to use Internet access. When you install a program that uses the Internet, you may be asked to approve the connection the first time. The safest practice is to reject online connections that you don't initiate or recognize.

- **Windows Update:** See the "Install Optional Updates" section for information on Windows Update.

- **Virus Protection:** Having virus protection for your computer is essential. Windows Defender provides antivirus protection, although you can install some other antivirus program.

- **Spyware and Unwanted Software Protection:** If this service is on, you have basic protection from malicious software provided by Windows Defender.

- **Internet Security Settings:** These settings pertain to your browser. The default settings may be adequate. To learn more, see the following tip.

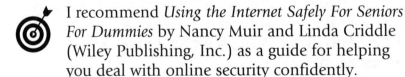 I recommend *Using the Internet Safely For Seniors For Dummies* by Nancy Muir and Linda Criddle (Wiley Publishing, Inc.) as a guide for helping you deal with online security confidently.

- **User Account Control (UAC):** This function notifies you of programs that try to make changes to your system and requires that you confirm any such changes. In particular, UAC lets you know when a program tries to run or install software that may be malicious. When in doubt, say No or Cancel to UAC messages.

- **Windows SmartScreen:** This function blocks you from downloading programs, except through the Microsoft Store, as well as files capable of changing your system maliciously.

- **Network Access Protection (NAP):** If this service is off, that isn't a problem, unless the computer connects to a business network. NAP protects a business network from machines that aren't updated and secure.

- **Windows Activation:** Windows 8 must be activated soon after the first time you use it. The activation process connects to the Internet and exchanges information automatically with Microsoft.

4. Select the Maintenance heading to see what that section includes. Functions under Maintenance consist of the following:

- **Check for solutions to problem reports:** This setting is on, allowing Windows 8 to regularly check for solutions to problems it uncovers.

- **Automatic Maintenance:** Your computer automatically performs critical updates, security scans, and diagnostics each day.

 If your computer is in a guest room or bedroom, you may want to change the Automatic Maintenance setting to run maintenance tasks at some time other than the default 3:00 a.m. Your computer may actually wake up at that hour for maintenance, unless you use a power strip to turn off the computer after

shutting down. If the computer can't run maintenance at the appointed hour, it will do so at the next
opportunity.

- **HomeGroup:** A *homegroup* is network that allows
  you to share files and printers between two or
  more computers. See Chapter 14 for information
  on networks, including homegroups.

- **File History:** See Chapter 15 for information on
  using the File History option, which is off by
  default.

- **Drive status:** *Drives* refers to hard disks inside or
  attached to your computer. Your documents, photos, and Windows 8 itself are stored on one or
  more drives. Ideally, the drive status is *All drives are
  working properly*. See Chapter 15 for information
  on backing up and restoring files.

Action Center is a troubleshooting tool, so you
should check it if you have problems running
Windows 8.

5. Under Check for Solutions to Problem Reports, select
View Reliability History. The Reliability Monitor screen
graphs your computer's stability and indicates hardware
and software problems, including those you may not be
aware of. In **Figure 12-3**, note the critical events (*crashes*)
on 4/12/12 and 4/19/12, as indicated by the white *x* in a
red circle. Blue circles are information about software
installation and updates. Yellow triangles are warnings
about noncritical events — something that didn't crash
the computer. Select a day in the graph to display details
in the lower portion of the screen. In **Figure 12-3**, one of
the critical events involved File Explorer, which stopped
responding (froze or crashed). The time of the event
(12:04 PM) may be useful in determining what else was
going on when File Explorer crashed.

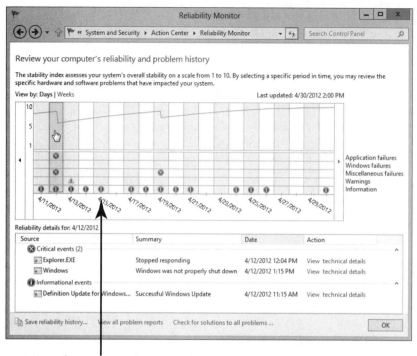

Select for more information
Figure 12-3

 Reviewing the Reliability Monitor screen will help you distinguish between a one-time glitch and a recurring or worsening problem.

Install Optional Updates

1. In the System window (refer to **Figure 12-1**), select Windows Update in the lower-left corner. Windows Update appears on the desktop, as shown in **Figure 12-4**. (See Chapter 5 for information about working with the desktop.)

 Critical updates are installed automatically. Optional updates are just that — optional. Note, however, that optional updates may apply to computer hardware, such as your monitor or printer, and may improve performance or fix problems with devices.

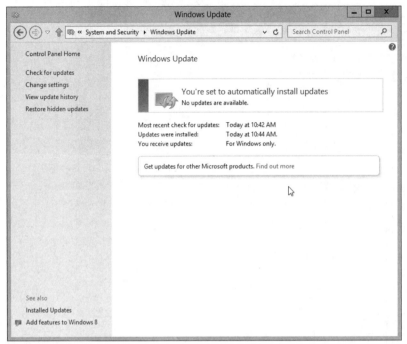

Figure 12-4

2. In **Figure 12**-4, no updates are available. Your results may be different. Note the following information listed on the screen:

- **Most Recent Check for Updates:** The date and time when Windows 8 checked for updates, which should be the current day or very recent. If the most recent check is more than a week old, select the Check for Updates link on the left.

- **Updates Were Installed:** The date and time when Windows 8 was last updated. If you want to know what update was performed, select View Update History.

- **You Receive Updates:** Initially, Windows Update is for Windows 8 only. See the section "Get Updates for Other Microsoft Programs," later in this chapter.

3. If you see a link indicating that you have optional
updates available, select that link. The Select Updates to
Install window appears, as shown in **Figure 12-5**. To
learn more about an update, select its name. The area to
the right then displays information for the selected
update. Select the More Information link if you want to
know even more.

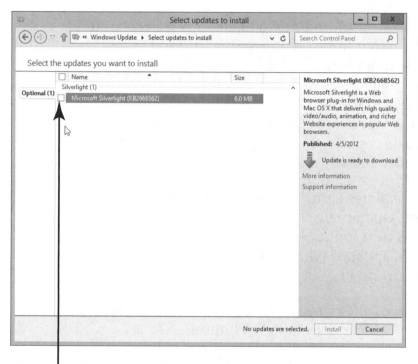

Select updates to install
Figure 12-5

 Note whether the update description includes a
warning (marked by an exclamation point in a circle)
that you may need to restart your computer after
installing the update. In most cases, you won't have
to restart immediately; you can shut down at the end
of the day and start normally the next day.

4. Select the check box next to any or all updates you want to install. Then select the Install button. You can return to the Start screen and do other things during installation, but don't close this window or shut down your computer until the screen indicates installation is complete.

Get Updates for Other Microsoft Programs

1. If you use Microsoft software other than Windows — in particular, Word (for word processing) or Excel (spreadsheet app) — you can have Windows Update check for updates to those programs, as well. In the desktop Windows Update screen (refer to **Figure 12-4**), select the Find Out More link next to Get Updates for Other Microsoft Products. If you don't see this option, the choice to check for additional updates may already be selected (see Step 5).

2. Internet Explorer launches and automatically browses the Microsoft Update site shown in **Figure 12-6**. Select the check box next to I Agree to the Terms of Use for Microsoft Update. (What choice do you have, really?) Then select Install.

3. If User Account Control requires you to confirm running Windows Update, select the Yes button.

4. A web page indicates that Microsoft Update was successfully installed. Select the X in the upper-right corner to close the browser window.

5. Windows Update automatically starts and searches for updates. If Windows Update doesn't start, select Check for Updates, on the left side of the Windows Update screen. Note that the You Receive Updates option now states For Windows and Other Products from Microsoft Update.

6. If updates are found and you want to install them, continue with Steps 3 and 4 in the preceding section.

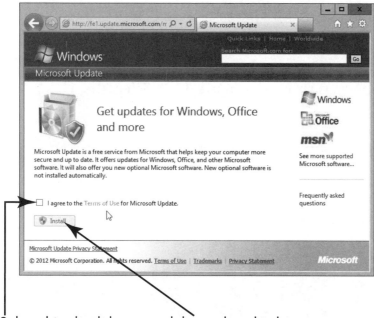

Select this check box...and then select this button
Figure 12-6

Install a New Program on the Desktop

1. You can install software that you download from the Web or from a CD or DVD for use on the desktop. (Windows 8 apps must be installed through the Microsoft Store.) In this set of steps, you install Windows Photo Gallery, my favorite free program for editing photos. To install Photo Gallery, first switch to the desktop. Select the blue *e* in the taskbar to run Microsoft Internet Explorer (MSIE). Enter **get.live.com** in the address bar. (See Chapter 6 for information on using Microsoft Internet Explorer.)

 You can also get Windows Photo Gallery by selecting a link on the Welcome, Readers page of the book's website (www.win8mjh.com).

 If a website offers to install a program automatically, look at that suggestion with suspicion. It may be legitimate or it may be malevolent. Decline downloads from sources that you don't know and trust already.

2. On the Windows Essentials web page, select Photo Gallery. On the Photo Gallery page, select Download Now.

3. Internet Explorer displays a message at the bottom of the browser window, as shown in **Figure 12-7.** Select the Run button.

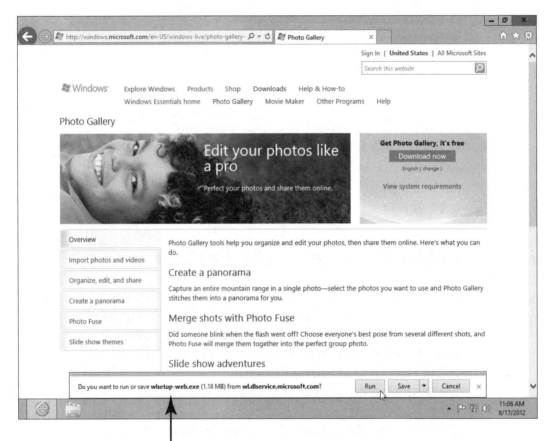

Internet Explorer message

Figure 12-7

4. Note that Internet Explorer displays a progress indicator at the bottom of the browser window. When the download is complete, Internet Explorer performs a security

scan of the program. Then, the User Account Control asks for confirmation to continue with the installation. Select the Yes button.

5. The Windows Essentials screen appears. Select Choose the Programs You Want to Install. On the Select Programs to Install screen, deselect everything except Photo Gallery and Movie Maker (one option) and Microsoft SkyDrive, a useful tool for accessing storage on the Web (*cloud storage*). Then, select Install.

 Generally, if the installer for a program offers Express or Custom installation options, choose the Express option to let the installer set up the program without further input from you. The Custom or Advanced Settings option allows you to specify where to install the program and, perhaps, which parts of the program to install.

6. A moving bar indicates the progress of the installation, which should take a few minutes. On the screen that indicates installation is done, select the Close button.

 Many programs try to connect to the Internet for updates during installation or when you run the installed program. The first time you run a program, you may be asked if you want to register the program or configure some aspect of the program. Go with the default (assumed) responses, if you're not sure.

7. To run Photo Gallery, switch to the Start screen and scroll to the right to find the Photo Gallery tile. Select that tile, and Photo Gallery opens on the desktop. If you see the Sign In with Your Email Address screen, enter your Microsoft Account e-mail address and password, select Remember My ID and Password, and then select Sign In. (Or select Cancel.)

8. Photo Gallery, like the Photo app, displays photos from your Photo Library. For steps on using Photo Gallery to tag, flag, rate, or edit photos, see the book's website (www.win8mjh.com).

 To install a program that comes on a CD or DVD, insert the program disc into your computer's disc drive or tray, label side up (or, if your computer has a vertical disc slot, insert the disc with the label side facing left). The AutoPlay dialog box appears. Select the option to run Install or Setup. User Account Control may ask if you really want to run this program. (Windows 8 tries to keep you from installing software unintentionally by asking for confirmation.)

Remove Desktop Programs

1. Unlike Windows 8 apps from the Microsoft Store, desktop programs are installed and uninstalled directly through the desktop itself. To see which desktop programs are installed, select Control Panel Home on the System, Action Center, or Windows Update screen. See the first section in this chapter, "Explore System Information on the Desktop," for steps.

 Most of the functions covered in this chapter are part of Control Panel, which presents many functions for tweaking your computer setup. You can also access Control Panel through the Settings charm while on the desktop.

2. In the Control Panel window (shown in **Figure 12-8**), under Programs, select Uninstall a Program. (You don't have to uninstall anything; you can simply see what the option offers.)

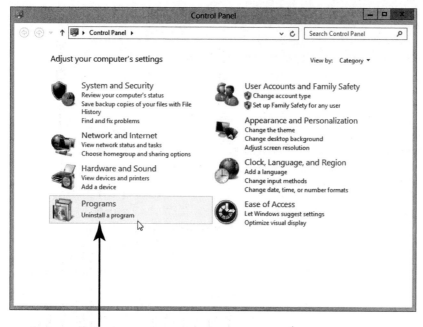

Uninstall a program or just look

Figure 12-8

3. The Programs and Features window lists desktop programs, not Windows 8 apps. Initially, these programs are sorted by name. You may want to see the date you last used each program because a program you haven't used in ages may be a safe one to remove. (Otherwise, skip to Step 5.) Use one of the following techniques to display the date last used:

- **Mouse:** Move the mouse pointer over any column heading, such as Name. Click the right mouse button.

- **Touchscreen:** Tap and hold down on any column heading, such as Name. When a box appears around your fingertip, lift your finger.

4. On the context menu that appears, select More. In the Chose Details window (shown in **Figure 12-9**), select Last Used On, and then select the OK button. The Last Used On column appears to the right of all the other columns.

 Unfortunately, Last Used On may be blank. In fact, even if you just used Photo Gallery in the previous section, nothing appears in the Last Used On column.

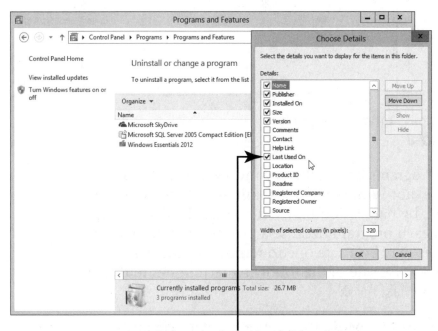

Select the Last Used On option

Figure 12-9

5. To change a program, select it. For this example, select Windows Essentials, as shown in **Figure 12-10**. You don't have to uninstall Photo Gallery, but if you do, you can follow the steps in the preceding section to reinstall it.

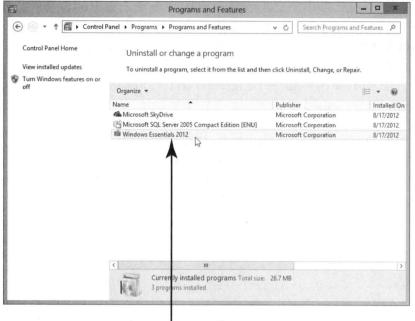

Select to uninstall

Figure 12-10

6. Select the Uninstall/Change button, if necessary. The Windows Essentials screen offers options to Remove One or More or to Repair All. Some programs will offer an option to Change the program as well. Repair or Change may be useful for a desktop program that you want to keep but isn't running as expected. Select Remove One or More Windows Essential Programs or Cancel. If you selected Remove, select Photo Gallery on the next screen, then select Uninstall. (Your photos are not removed.)

7. If you uninstalled Photo Gallery or another program, it will no longer appear in the Programs and Features window or on the Start screen.

Just because you can uninstall a program doesn't mean you should. You can simply ignore programs you don't use. Look at a program's name, publisher, and date installed to determine whether you actually use a program. You may recognize a program you installed recently, as opposed to one installed before you got your computer. If you find that it's more productive to remove large programs than small ones, repeat Steps 3 and 4 to group by size.

 Before you uninstall a program that you may want to reinstall later, make sure that you have a copy of it on a CD or DVD (or that you know where to download it from the Web again). You have no undo option when you uninstall a program.

Connecting a Printer and Other Devices

*E*very computer has a screen. Most computers, other than tablets, also have a keyboard and a mouse or other pointing device. You can add a mouse to a laptop that lacks one or replace the keyboard or mouse that came with your computer. Add a printer or a scanner to extend your computer's functionality.

You can even add a second screen, and use Windows 8 apps and the desktop simultaneously. Laptops have built-in support for two displays — an external display in addition to the laptop screen — and Windows 8 makes it easy to use a second display. Many desktop computers also support a second display.

For any hardware add-ons — which tech-folk call *peripherals* — Windows 8 has a trick up its sleeve. Thanks to *plug and play* technology, which automatically identifies add-on devices, connecting new devices to your computer can be quite easy.

In this chapter, you explore the devices connected to your computer, as well as options available for those devices. You also find out how to add a printer and a second screen.

Trust USB Plug and Play for Hardware

You may find many kinds of add-on devices useful:

➠ A **printer** lets you, well, print documents and photos. Your choices for printers include black and white versus color, and inkjet versus laser printer. Multifunction printers also work as a copier, scanner, and fax machine.

➠ A **digital camera** captures photos that you can copy to your computer to enjoy and to share with others. See Chapter 10 for information on working with photos.

➠ A **scanner** enables you to make digital images of old photos or documents so that you can view them on-screen.

➠ An **external hard drive** stores backup copies of your files. See Chapter 15 for information on adding a hard drive to your computer.

➠ An additional or replacement **pointing device** (your mouse is a pointing device), including a trackball or a pen with a tablet, may be more comfortable to use than what came with your computer. Switching between pointing devices helps you avoid repetitive stress. A wireless mouse eliminates the hassle of dealing with a cord. Some people like to add a mouse as an alternative to their laptop's built-in touchpad.

➠ A **microphone** is crucial for communicating by voice with your computer, through speech recognition, or with your friends over the Internet. A combination headset with microphone may produce the clearest sound.

➠ A **video camera** (or *webcam*) is essential for video phone calls *a la* the Jetsons. See Chapter 10 for information on using a webcam.

The majority of these devices connect using *USB* (Universal Serial Bus) technology. When you connect a device to your computer using a USB cable to the USB port (see **Figure 13-1**), the device identifies itself to the computer. This identification process is called *plug and play*. Ideally, you connect your device, and it simply works.

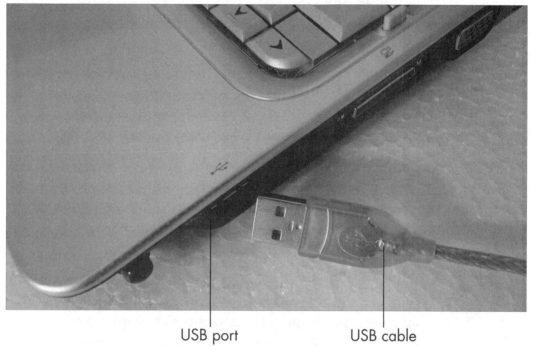

USB port   USB cable

Figure 13-1

Windows 8 uses a *device driver* to communicate with an add-on device. The driver is really a program that tells Windows 8 how to run the device. When you connect a device, such as a printer, Windows 8 looks for a driver (in this case, a *printer driver*). That driver may be built into Windows 8, come on a disc that's packaged with the device, or need to be downloaded from the Internet, either automatically by Windows 8 or manually by you.

 Every computer has at least a couple of USB ports. Some are in the front, and others are in the back of the computer and harder to reach. If your computer doesn't have enough ports, you can add more by buying a USB hub, which is a small box with two to four USB ports. If a port is hard to reach with a device's cable, you can buy a USB extension cable. Office supply stores may have hubs and cables.

 Bluetooth is a wireless technology for adding devices to your computer. If your computer has Bluetooth, you can use Bluetooth as well as USB to add some devices, especially a microphone or headset.

See All Devices

1. On the Start screen, type **devices**. Select Settings in the Search panel, then Devices in the search results on the left. The Devices category of PC Settings appears, as shown in **Figure 13-2**.

 To search using a touchscreen, swipe from the right edge to display the charms bar. Select the Search charm. Then select in the search box to display the virtual keyboard.

 Are you wondering why you don't use the prominent Devices charm on the charms bar to see all devices? That charm shows only those devices appropriate to a specific app. On the Start screen, the Devices panel displays *Start can't send to any devices* or *There's nothing to send right now*. That doesn't mean you don't have any devices, just that none are available to the Start screen.

2. Note the specific devices that appear on the right, in alphabetical order. Devices listed may include your monitor, speakers, headphones, keyboard, mouse, and more. Devices shared through your homegroup or network also appear here. For information on adjusting device settings, see the "Access Device Options on the Desktop" section, later in the chapter.

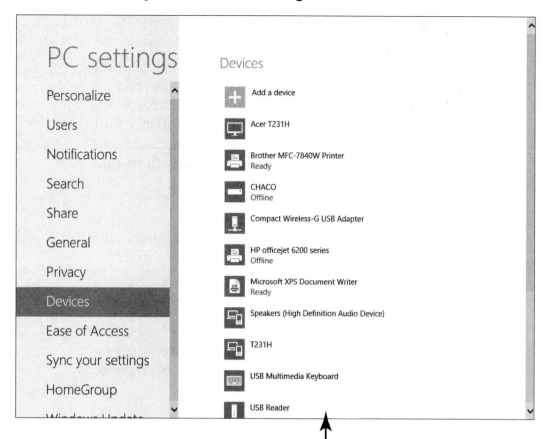

List of printers, screens, and more

Figure 13-2

 Some, but not all, devices display information below the device name. A network device may display *Offline* (not accessible) or may display nothing if it is accessible. A printer may display *Ready* or may display nothing if the printer isn't ready.

 You are unlikely to need the Add a Device button because most devices are added *automagically* (that's a word nerds like to use). However, if you select Add a Device, Windows 8 scans for additional hardware. No harm in doing so.

Connect a Printer or Other Device

1. Take your printer out of the box. Keep all the packing material together until you know you won't need to return the printer. Arrange all the components for easy access. In addition to the printer, you'll probably find ink cartridges or a toner cartridge, a power cable, and a CD with printer software. Read the setup instructions that come with your printer.

 Some of these steps apply to other devices, such as a mouse, a webcam, or a microphone. Printers often have more packaging and require more assembly than other devices.

2. Remove all tape from the printer. Most printers ship with the print mechanism locked in place to prevent it from moving during shipping. Look for brightly colored tape, paper, or plastic indicating what you need to move or remove to release the print mechanism.

3. Put the printer within cable length of your computer. Insert the ink or toner cartridge before you turn on the printer for the first time. Place some paper in the paper drawer or tray. Connect the printer to the power supply. Plug the printer cable into the printer and into the computer.

 Your printer may have come with a disc with a printer driver and other software. You don't need that disc unless Windows 8 fails to correctly install a driver automatically.

4. Turn on the printer. You may see some informational messages as Windows 8 handles the configuration.

5. To confirm that your printer is installed properly, see the preceding section, "See All Devices."

Access Device Options on the Desktop

1. For more control over device setup, search for **devices** on the Start screen. Select Settings in the Search panel. On the left, select Devices and Printers to display the window shown in **Figure 13-3**.

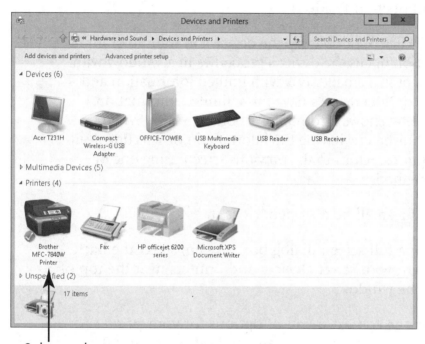

Select a device to access options

Figure 13-3

2. The Device and Printers window shows the devices attached to your computer, including the computer itself, the display (or monitor), external add-on devices (such as a hard drive, flash drive, or memory card), and the mouse.

 Most of these devices also appear in the Devices category of PC Settings. However, you'll find options under Devices and Printer that aren't available in PC Settings, such as settings for devices.

Windows 8 automatically installs the Microsoft XPS Document Writer. This device doesn't print but does create files you could print later using a real printer. For example, if you're in a coffee shop and want to print a web page or an e-mail message, you could use this device and then open the file it creates when your computer is connected to a printer. (That file will open in Reader.)

3. Double-click or double-tap the device you want to examine. This action opens the device's properties in a window with options or in a smaller box with limited information and options. (Older devices have more limited information.) **Figure 13-4** shows information about a printer. When you're finished reviewing the information or selecting available options, return to the previous screen using one of these methods:

- If a small box is open, close it.

- If a full-screen dialog box is open, select the back arrow or select Devices and Printers near the top of the window.

4. Display the context menu of options for your printer (or any device) using one of these methods (use the XPS device if you don't have another printer): Click the right mouse button or tap and hold until you see a small box appear under your finger and then release. Select Printer Properties from the menu. (Oddly, the menu also has a separate Properties option — be sure to select Printer Properties, instead.)

Some devices offer several options

Figure 13-4

5. In the Properties window, select the Print Test Page button. Another window opens indicating *A test page has been sent to your printer*. Select Close.

If a test page doesn't print, check that both ends of the cable are plugged in properly and make sure the printer is turned on. Try to print a test page again. For more help, contact the printer manufacturer or the store where you bought the printer, or search the Web.

If you're having problems with any device, select the Troubleshoot option on the context menu to open a guided troubleshooting program that will walk you through options for resolving problems with the device.

The top of the Device and Printers window has the Add Devices and Printers button, but you need to use it only if Windows 8 doesn't automatically detect and install your device. With USB and plug and play, most devices install automatically.

Calibrate Your Touchscreen

1. If you have a problem accurately selecting objects on your screen using touch, you can calibrate your screen alignment. On the Start screen, type **touch**. Select the Settings category in the Search panel. Then select Calibrate the Screen for Pen or Touch Input.

2. In the Tablet PC Settings window, select the Calibrate button, as shown in **Figure 13-5**. User Account Control may ask you to confirm that you want to run the Digitizer Calibration Tool. If so, select Yes.

Figure 13-5

If your touchscreen is badly calibrated, you may not be able to tap the Calibrate button. In that case, plug in a mouse to make the selection, and then continue using touch.

 Ignore the option to Choose the Order in Which Your Screen Rotates. Windows 8 tablets automatically rotate the screen content as you turn the tablet. Look for the orientation lock on your tablet. If orientation lock is on, the screen will not rotate between portrait (vertical) and landscape (horizontal).

3. The screen displays lines around its perimeter, forming a box near the edge of the screen and a second box inside the first about half an inch from the edge. Lines connect these boxes near each corner. The result is 16 intersections. Starting at the upper-left corner, use your finger or a stylus to tap each intersection, which displays two short black lines forming crosshairs. As you touch each intersection, Windows 8 adjusts settings according to your touch. If that touch is accepted, the crosshairs move to the next intersection to the right. If not, tap the previous intersection again. As the crosshairs move, tap the highlighted intersection, left to right, down, then left to right again. The process takes much longer to read about than to do.

 If Windows 8 doesn't recognize your touch, it won't continue with the process. The screen says *Right-click anywhere to return to the last calibration point*. What if you don't have a mouse? Tap and hold until you see the little box under your fingertip, and then release — that's the touch equivalent of a click of the right mouse button.

4. After you have selected each of the 16 calibration points in turn, a box pops up asking whether or not you want to save the calibration data. Select OK unless you think something went wrong. In that case, select Cancel.

 It's unlikely but possible that you can't continue to the end of the process. If so, the screen says *Press the Esc button to close the tool*. What if you don't have a keyboard? In that case, press and hold the Windows button (with the four-part Windows logo) on the tablet edge as you also press the power button, and then release both. On the next screen, select Task Manager. In the Task Manager window, select Digitizer Calibration Tool, and then select the End Task button. Makes one yearn for an Esc.

Add a Second Screen for Twice the Fun

1. Before you buy a second screen (also called a *monitor*), you should find out whether your computer is ready for it. On the Start screen, type **second**. Select the Settings category in the Search panel. Then select Project to a Second Screen. The Second Screen panel slides into view.

 The keyboard shortcut for the Second Screen panel is ⊞+P (for *projector*).

2. If you see *Your PC can't project to another screen*, you can't do more without significant changes to your graphics hardware.

 Most laptops and some tablets support a second screen, which is a great option when you want a screen larger than the first.

3. If you see the options shown in **Figure 13-6**, you can connect a second screen. If you have a relatively new TV, you may be able to connect your computer and TV using only a cable (a really long cable if the devices are in different rooms). You also have the option of buying a second monitor or a TV with a connection for a computer.

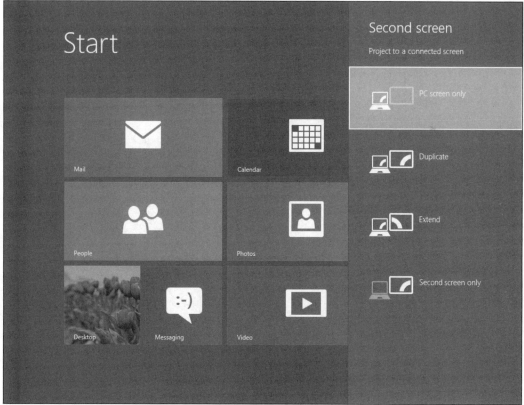

Figure 13-6

 The best option for connecting is HDMI because it can transmit sound as well as video, allowing you to watch and listen to video on a TV. Both devices require HDMI connections, as well as an HDMI cable. The HDMI alternative is VGA connections and cable, suitable for a non-TV monitor.

4. To connect a second display, plug your second display into the wall or a power strip and connect the cable to your computer. See **Figure 13-7** for an example of a VGA display cable and plug (this is not USB). On a desktop computer, the plug is behind the computer. Your first display will be plugged in near the plug for the second. On a laptop or tablet, the plug is located along one of the edges. Turn the second screen on.

Display port   Display plug

Figure 13-7

5. Repeat Step 1 to display the Second Screen panel (refer to **Figure 13-6**). Note each of these options:

- **PC Screen Only** is the default setting. The second screen is unused.

- **Duplicate** places the same content on both screens. This is the easiest setting to adjust to because it doesn't make a difference which screen you look at — except that one of them is your big screen TV.

- **Extend** adds the extra screen space to the first screen as if it were all one big screen (oddly separated into two pieces). Using Extend, you can see the Start screen and your Windows 8 apps on either screen and the desktop simultaneously on the other. This may be the best setting for desktop users to get the most out of two screens on a regular basis.

- **Second Screen Only** turns off the original computer screen. Not recommended unless you want to use the second screen exclusively.

6. Select Duplicate. Everything on your original computer screen also appears on the second screen. Go pop some popcorn while you see Chapter 10 for information on displaying photos and Chapter 11 for information on watching videos. That's entertainment, twenty-first-century style.

Organizing Your Documents

*E*verything inside your computer is stored on a disk. Your computer has a primary disk, formally called the internal *hard drive.* You may see this disk referred to as the C: drive. (The terms *drive* and *disk* are interchangeable.)

The contents of a disk are organized into individual files. When you save a document, you create a file on a disk. Many other files on the disk belong to the programs you use, including the thousands of files that make up Windows 8.

Disks also are organized into *folders,* which are containers for files. For its own files, Windows 8 has a main folder that contains dozens of other folders (called *subfolders*). One extra-important folder has the same name as your user name, which you created the first time you turned on the computer (see Chapter 1). Inside or below that user account folder, Windows 8 creates more folders to help you organize your files by type. For example, all your photos go into the Pictures folder, and all your documents go into the Documents folder.

In this chapter, you search for files and explore your disk, folders, and documents. You work with File Explorer as you create new folders to organize documents and move files from one folder to another. You also copy files from your hard disk to other disks to take with you or give to other people. File management is much more exciting than it may sound so far.

Find a Misplaced File

1. To search for a misplaced file, begin on the Start screen. Type the name of a document or photo you have on your computer, for example, **read**. (In Chapter 6, you downloaded a file with *read* in its name.) On the search results screen, select Files, as shown in **Figure 14-1**.

Select the Files option

Figure 14-1

 To search using a touchscreen, swipe from the right edge to display the charms bar. Select the Search charm. Select in the search box to display the virtual keyboard.

 The keyboard shortcut for Search is ■+Q (for query).

2. To open a file found in Step 1, select that file. Then, close the app that opens that file using one of these methods:

- **Mouse:** Move the mouse pointer to the top of the screen. When the pointer changes to a hand symbol, click and hold down the left mouse button. Drag the app down until part of the app is off the bottom of the screen. Then release the left mouse button to close the app and return to the Start screen.

- **Touchscreen:** Swipe down from the top of the screen until part of the app is off the bottom of the screen. Then lift your finger to close the app and return to the Start screen.

- **Keyboard:** Press Alt+F4.

Strictly speaking, if you find what you're looking for, stop looking. (No extra charge for pearls of wisdom.) In this case, however, keep looking because doing so reveals important information about how files are organized and how you can take control of that organization.

3. On the Start screen, select the Desktop tile. On the desktop, select the File Explorer icon (the yellow folder) in the taskbar. File Explorer opens. Note the *ribbon*, which is the collapsible toolbar at the top of the window, as shown in **Figure** 14-2.

Collapse or expand the ribbon

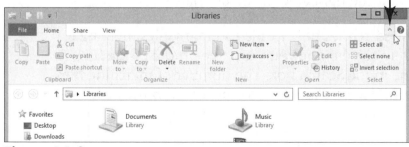

Figure 14-2

On the ribbon, tools are grouped by tabs, which in File Explorer consist of File, Home, Share, and View, as well as other tabs that appear based on the selection. Tabs are further divided into sections, labeled below the related tools. (Note, for example, the Clipboard section on the Home tab.) To expand the ribbon, select the up arrow at the far right of the tabs. Collapse the ribbon by selecting the down arrow. Select a tab to display its tools, whether the ribbon is expanded or collapsed.

4. Select the box labeled *Search* (probably followed by *Libraries*), below the ribbon and to the right. Type **read** (or the name of a file you found in Step 1). As you type, File Explorer displays any matching files, highlighting the text that matches. **Figure 14-3** shows the results of a search for *read* on my computer.

Type your search item

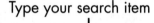
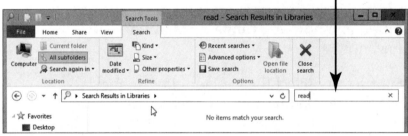

Figure 14-3

 On a touchscreen, the virtual keyboard doesn't appear on the desktop until you select the keyboard icon on the right side of the taskbar.

 If the search results include too many files, making it hard to see the one you want, type more of the file name in the Search box. The number of matching files should decrease as you type more text in the box.

5. Note that in **Figure 14-1**, I found a file, but not so in **Figure 14-3**. This is due to *focus* — where File Explorer is searching, which is in the libraries. (Why does Colonel Mustard spring to mind?) *Libraries* are home to most of your files and are divided into four specific libraries: Documents, Music, Pictures, and Videos. Libraries contain folders and files. Visualize the organization from larger to smaller as Disks > Libraries > Folders > Files. But my *read* file isn't in any of my libraries. The *read* file is in a folder called Downloads, because I downloaded it in Chapter 6.

 You can use Search Tools in the ribbon to refine a search, as needed. Start a search, and then select the Search tab. In the section labeled Refine, select Date Modified and then select a time period ranging from Today to Last Year. Select Kind to limit the search to specific types of files. You can even select by size and other properties.

6. On the left side of Explorer, select the Downloads folder under Favorites. Even if you see the file with read in its name, type **read** in the *Search Downloads* box for practice in finding a file. (Or select Recent Searches in the ribbon, and then select the file name for which you're searching.)

 If you can't find a file, select Computer on the left, and repeat Step 4. This action searches the entire computer, which takes longer and turns up some irrelevant files along with the missing one (you hope!).

Use Libraries for Easy Access to Files

1. On the desktop, select the File Explorer icon in the task-bar. The right side of Explorer is called the *content area*. The left side of Explorer is called the *navigation pane* and contains five sections. Explorer starts with its focus on the *Libraries* section. Under Libraries, select Documents; note any files displayed on the right.

> If you see libraries or folders on the left and right, note that selecting and opening on the left only requires a single click or tap, whereas selecting on the right requires one click or tap to select and a second in quick succession to open.

> The keyboard shortcut to open File Explorer is ⊞+E. You don't need to switch to the desktop before using the shortcut.

2. On the left, select Music, then Pictures, and then Videos, while noting the files in each library on the right. Select Documents again.

3. To create a practice document you can use in later sections, select the Home tab in the ribbon. In the New section, select New Item, and then select Text Document, as shown in **Figure 14-4**. (If you don't see this option, make sure that the Documents library is selected.) An empty text document is created and the words *New Text Document* are highlighted so you can type a new name. Type **practice file**. (You'll rename this file in a later section.) Feel free to repeat this step to create additional items for practice, including Rich Text Documents or Bitmap Images.

> On a touchscreen, the virtual keyboard doesn't appear on the desktop until you select the keyboard icon on the right side of the taskbar.

Select New Item to create an empty document

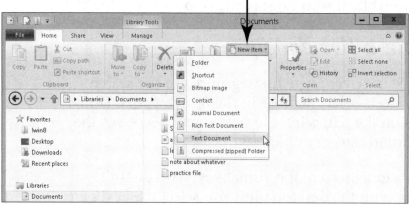

Figure 14-4

4. Select the View tab in the ribbon. In the Layout section, select each option, such as Extra Large Icons and Large, Medium, and Small Icons. If you see a downward-pointing triangle on the right edge of the Layout options, select that triangle to display even more options. Try them all, if you like.

 Certain layouts are better for certain purposes. For example, photos are easier to recognize as Extra Large Icons than as a List. **Figure 14-5** shows my documents using the Details view, which includes the date the file was modified.

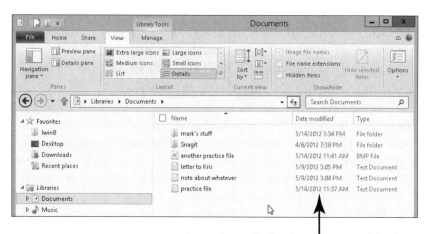

Details include the date modified

Figure 14-5

The more time you spend in File Explorer, the more worthwhile it is to explore the ribbon as you need it.

Create or Join a Homegroup

1. On the Start screen, type **homegroup**. On the search results screen, select Settings in the Search panel. Under Settings on the left, select HomeGroup. This opens the HomeGroup category of PC Settings.

On a touchscreen, the virtual keyboard doesn't appear on the desktop until you select the keyboard icon on the right side of the taskbar.

A *homegroup* is a simple *network*, which is a connection between two or more computers for the purpose of sharing resources, such as an Internet connection, files, printers, and storage. One user on a network creates a homegroup that other users join, if they choose.

You can also create or join a homegroup by selecting Homegroup in the navigation pane of File Explorer.

2. If *A Homegroup Is Available* appears on screen, select the Enter Homegroup Password box. Type the password and select Join.

The person who created the homegroup can give you the password. If that person doesn't remember it, he or she can follow the steps in this section on his or her own machine to get the password for you.

If you see *HomeGroup Is Only Available on a Home Network*, jump to the "Browse for a Network" section, later in this chapter.

3. If you are the first person to use this function in your household or you have already joined a homegroup, the right side of the screen displays the Libraries and Devices section.

4. For each library that you want to share in the Libraries and Devices section, shown in **Figure 14-6**, click or tap to the right of the small black box in the rectangular slider. Separate options control the sharing of printers and devices (including disks) and allow media devices (such as the Microsoft Xbox game console) to play your music, pictures, or videos.

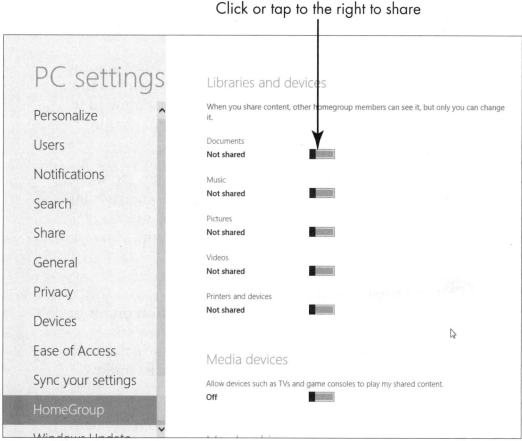

Figure 14-6

Libraries and devices shared in the homegroup will appear in the file picker and other places where you save or open files, including File Explorer.

 If you want to turn off sharing for a library, click or tap to the left of the black box that appears in the rectangular slider.

5. Scroll down, if necessary, to see the Membership section. The password required by other users to join your homegroup appears in the box.

 Although you can change this password through a long series of steps, you'll use this password only when a computer joins a homegroup for the first time.

 In the unlikely event that you want to leave a homegroup, select the Leave button at the bottom of the Libraries and Devices screen. I don't recommend this because doing so removes all options for sharing through HomeGroup.

6. Switch to the desktop and open File Explorer. On the left, select Homegroup. If you have created or joined a homegroup, you'll see your computer and others that have joined. By selecting objects in the homegroup, you can access anything shared by others.

Browse for a Network

1. On the Start screen, type **network**. On the search results screen, select the Network app. The Network window opens on the desktop.

 To search using a touchscreen, swipe from the right edge to display the charms bar. Select the Search charm. Then select in the search box to display the virtual keyboard.

2. In the Network window, you may see icons for other computers on your network, as well as your own. My network is shown in **Figure** 14-7. Your screen may show only two or three computers. Select one of the other computers. Shared resources will appear in the window. (You may be asked for a user name and password, obtainable from the user of that computer.)

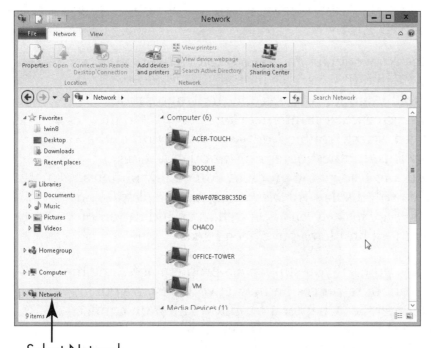

Select Network

Figure 14-7

 The difference between a homegroup and a network is subtle. A homegroup is specific kind of network and may be easier to create than a network. A network has more options and can give you finer control over access to sharing. Take the easy route: Use an existing homegroup or network or create a homegroup.

3. If you see the message *Network discovery and file sharing are turned off. Network computers and devices are not visible. Click to change…* just below the ribbon, select that message. Then select Turn On Network Discovery and File Sharing on the pop-up menu. This option enables your computer to find other computers and to be found by others.

 If you're on a public network, don't turn on network discovery.

4. Select the Network tab, and then select Network and Sharing Center. If *Access type* indicates *No network access*, select Troubleshoot Problems. On the Troubleshoot Problems screen, select Internet Connections. On the next screen, select Troubleshoot My Connection to the Internet. This troubleshooter runs through a series of diagnostics to resolve the problem. After a few minutes, the screen will display *Troubleshooting has completed*. You may then see *Problems found*, as well as an indication of whether those problems have been fixed.

 At this point, if you still have a problem accessing the network or resources on the network, restart your computer. See Chapter 4 for information on connecting to the Internet. See Chapter 12 for information on maintaining Windows 8.

Create a Folder to Organize Your Files

1. In the File Explorer navigation pane, select the Documents library.

2. On the Home tab, select the New Folder button. An icon for the new folder appears in the content area on the right, with the name *New folder* next to it and already selected (see **Figure 14-8**).

Select the New Folder button

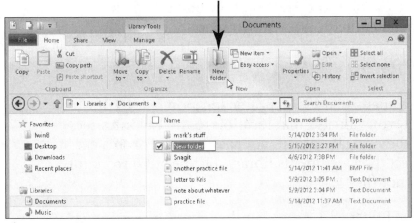

Figure 14-8

 On a touchscreen, the virtual keyboard doesn't appear on the desktop until you select the keyboard icon on the right side of the taskbar.

3. Type **practice folder** as the new name. Don't move the cursor or mouse before you start typing. Your new text will replace the highlighted text automatically. Press the Enter key to make the new name stick. (If you have a problem naming the folder, see the "Rename a File or a Folder" section, later in this chapter.)

4. Open your new folder by double-clicking or double-tapping its icon. The content area is empty.

5. To return to the Documents folder, select Documents in the navigation pane.

 Don't worry too much about creating folders, because the folders Windows 8 provides may be all you ever need. As you accumulate more files, however, placing them into other folders may help you stay organized. In the Documents library, for example, you might create a folder called Finances for files related to income, expenses, and investments, and another folder called Family for family-related documents. Which folders to create and how to name them depend entirely on your own sense of order.

Add a Location to Favorites

1. If you frequently access a specific location using File Explorer, you can add that location to the Favorites section of the navigation pane for easy access. For this exercise, select the Documents library. (These steps work for folders, not files.)

2. Select the folder you created in the preceding section (or any other folder).

3. On the Home tab, select the Easy Access button. From the drop-down list, select Add to Favorites (see **Figure 14-9**). A *shortcut* to your selected location appears at the bottom of the Favorites section.

Select the Easy Access button

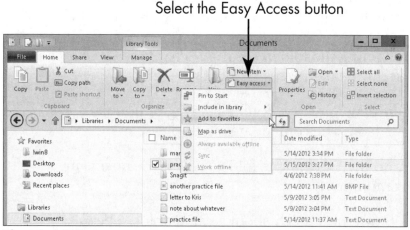

Figure 14-9

 To remove a shortcut from Favorites, select the Favorites heading, and then select the item you want to remove. Select the Delete button on the Home tab. This action deletes just the shortcut, not the original folder.

The Easy Access button also has an option to Pin to Start, which adds a tile for this location to the Start screen.

Use Check Boxes to Select Files

1. In File Explorer, you select files to move, copy, rename, or delete. You can add a check box to make selecting multiple files easier. In Explorer, select the View tab, and then select the Options button. The Folder Options window appears. Select the View tab (in the Folder Options window, not in the Explorer ribbon), as shown in **Figure 14-10**. Scroll through the Advanced Settings box until you see Use Check Boxes to Select Items, and then select that check box. Select the OK button.

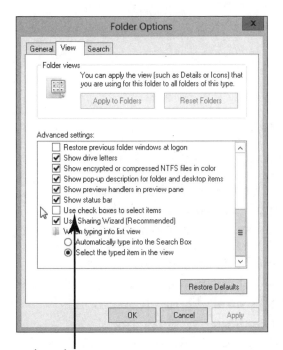

Select this option
Figure 14-10

2. Select the Documents library (or any library that contains more than one file). To select a file, click or tap the area to the left of the file name. (You won't see the check box until you select it with a tap or a click or hover over it with the mouse pointer.) Repeat to select additional files. If you want to deselect a file, select the check box again to remove the check mark. Close the window after you've seen how these check boxes work. **Figure 14-11** shows two selected files.

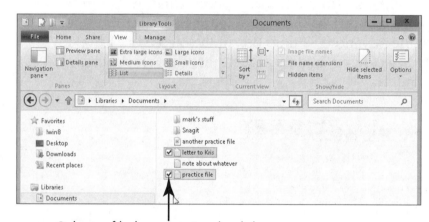

Select a file by using its check box

Figure 14-11

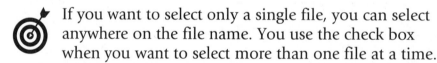 If you want to select only a single file, you can select anywhere on the file name. You use the check box when you want to select more than one file at a time.

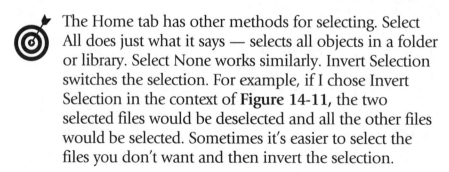 The Home tab has other methods for selecting. Select All does just what it says — selects all objects in a folder or library. Select None works similarly. Invert Selection switches the selection. For example, if I chose Invert Selection in the context of **Figure 14-11,** the two selected files would be deselected and all the other files would be selected. Sometimes it's easier to select the files you don't want and then invert the selection.

Add the Undo Button to File Explorer

1. You can add a button to File Explorer to undo an action, such as moving, renaming, or deleting a file. Above the Home tab, select the rather small down-pointing arrow to display the Customize Quick Access Toolbar list, as shown in **Figure 14-12**.

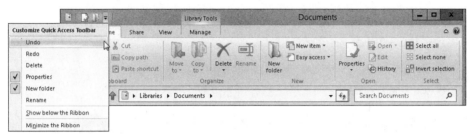

Figure 14-12

2. Select the Undo option from the drop-down list. The Undo button, which sports a blue arrow curving to the left, appears immediately to the left of the arrow you clicked in Step 1. You can undo most — but not all — actions in File Explorer by clicking or tapping this button immediately after the action. (Time isn't the issue. You can do something, and then undo it a year later if you don't do anything in the meantime.)

> The keyboard shortcut for undo is Ctrl+Z. This shortcut works regardless of whether the Undo button is on the screen.

> You may be able to undo a series of actions by repeating the undo function.

3. Select the Customize Quick Access Toolbar button again. Note that you can also add the Redo button, which, as you would expect, undoes the undo. All the other options appear also on larger buttons on the Home tab, so you don't need to add them to the Quick Access toolbar.

Move a File from One Folder to Another

1. You can move files to organize them. For this exercise, select the Documents library in File Explorer. Select one of your documents.

 To move more than one file at a time, see the section "Use Check Boxes to Select Files."

2. On the Home tab, select the Move To button, as shown in **Figure** 14-13.

Select the Move To button

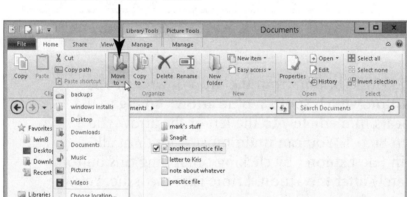

Figure 14-13

3. If you see the location you want in the drop-down list, you could select that location. However, for practice, select Choose Location. A window opens, showing every possible location. Select Libraries, then Documents, and then My Documents. Select the folder you created in the section "Create a Folder to Organize Your Files." (Or select the Make New Folder button and name that folder.) Finally, select the Move button, as shown in **Figure** 14-4.

Select a location

Figure 14-14

 Unless you move many files or large files, you may not see any indication that the move was completed.

4. In Explorer, select the folder to which you moved your file. There it is!

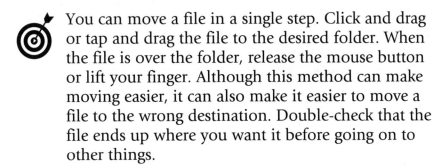 Note that the Copy To button works similarly, except the original file stays where it is and a copy is created in the new location.

Use these same steps to move a subfolder from one folder to another. However, don't move folders that Windows 8 creates.

You can move a file in a single step. Click and drag or tap and drag the file to the desired folder. When the file is over the folder, release the mouse button or lift your finger. Although this method can make moving easier, it can also make it easier to move a file to the wrong destination. Double-check that the file ends up where you want it before going on to other things.

Rename a File or a Folder

1. You can change the name of any file or folder you create. (Don't rename files in the Windows or Program Files folders.) For this exercise, select the Documents library in File Explorer. Then select one of your files.

 To rename more than one file at a time, see the section "Use Check Boxes to Select Files." On completion of the rename operation, the files you selected will share the name you provide; each file will have a unique number added to the name, starting with *(1)*.

2. On the Home tab, select the Rename button. In the content area, the current name of the file or folder is selected, as shown in **Figure 4-15**. If you type anything while the text is selected, you erase the current name, which is convenient if the new name is completely different from the old name. If you want to keep most of the current name and edit it, select inside the name or press the left- or right-arrow key to move to the place in the name where you want to type new text.

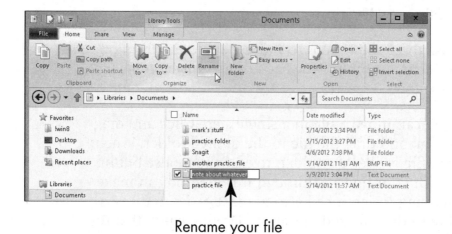

Rename your file

Figure 4-15

3. Type the new name, which can be more than 200 characters long (although a dozen characters may be more than
enough). You can capitalize letters and use spaces and
dashes, but you can't use slashes or asterisks, which
Windows 8 reserves for other purposes.

 On a touchscreen, the virtual keyboard doesn't
appear on the desktop until you select the keyboard
icon on the right side of the taskbar.

4. When you've typed the new name, press the Enter key to
finish the process.

Delete a File or Folder

1. You can delete any of your files you no longer need.
(Don't delete files in the Windows or Program Files fold-
ers.) For this exercise, select the Documents library in File
Explorer. Then select one your files.

 To delete more than one file at a time, see the section
"Use Check Boxes to Select Files."

2. On the Home tab, select the X on the Delete button.

 The keyboard shortcut to delete the selected file is the
Delete key (surprise!).

3. By default, Windows does not provide a confirmation
message — your file is gone with a click. A hundred files
can be deleted as easily. Select the bottom third of the
Delete button to display the drop-down list shown in
Figure 14-16. Select Show Recycle Confirmation.

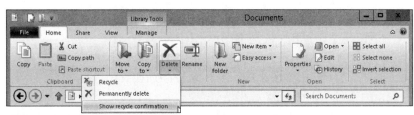

Figure 14-16

4. Select another file, and then select the X on the Delete button. The Delete File confirmation window appears. Select Yes to delete the file or No to cancel the operation.

 If the confirmation window seems unnecessary to you, repeat Step 3 to turn off the message.

 You can permanently delete a file, in which case it will not be in the Recycle Bin. Select the file, select the bottom of the Delete button, and then select the Permanently Delete option.

Get Back a File or Folder You Deleted

1. Normally, when you delete a file or folder, Windows 8 moves the object to the Recycle Bin. Objects remain in the Recycle Bin indefinitely, allowing you to restore something you deleted long after you did so. In File Explorer, select Desktop under Favorites. To open the Recycle Bin, double-click or double-tap the Recycle Bin in the content area.

 You can open the Recycle Bin also by double-clicking or double-tapping its icon on the desktop itself.

2. If many files or folders are listed in the Recycle Bin window, type the name of the item you want in the Search box in the top-right corner of the window. If any files match what you type, they will appear in the content area.

 On a touchscreen, the virtual keyboard doesn't appear on the desktop until you select the keyboard icon on the right side of the taskbar.

3. To restore a file or folder to its original location, select the file or folder in the Recycle Bin window. On the Manage tab, select Restore the Selected Items, as shown in **Figure 14-17.** The selected file or folder returns to the folder it was in before it was deleted.

Figure 14-17

 If Windows 8 needs disk space, it will automatically clear out the oldest files in the Recycle Bin first. If you want to get rid of everything in the Recycle Bin, select the Manage tab and then select Empty the Recycle Bin. After you empty the Recycle Bin, you can't undo your action.

 Don't select the Restore All Items button because it puts every single item in the Recycle Bin back in its original location. Most of the files in the Recycle Bin are probably files that you really meant to delete. Choosing this command would be like dumping the trash can on your living-room floor to find a penny you threw away.

 See Chapter 15 for information on backing up and restoring files.

Backing Up and Restoring Files

Some of your files — photos and documents — are priceless. If you accidentally delete a treasured file, what can you do but cry? You can insure your well-being by creating copies of your documents and photos.

The best insurance involves storing copies of files on devices separate from your computer. Such devices include the following:

⟹ **Flash drive and memory card:** Carry your files when you're away from your computer by storing them on a portable storage device. For example, you can store files on a USB *flash drive* (also called a *thumb drive*), which is about the size of a disposable cigarette lighter, or a *memory card*, which is the size of a postage stamp and is most often used in laptop computers and digital cameras. Common capacities for flash drives and memory cards range from 2 to 32GB.

 A *gigabyte* (GB) of storage can hold thousands of files, but you'll be amazed how quickly you can fill that space.

➠ **External hard drive:** This type of drive has a much higher capacity than a flash drive, making it ideal for backing up all your files — the best insurance. Affordable external hard drives range from 500GB to 3TB.

 A *terabytes* (TB) of storage is equal to a thousand gigabytes, which should be enough room to back up everything on your computer.

➠ **Network drive:** If your computer connects to a home network, you may be able to copy files to other devices on the network. For example, you could use a large capacity network drive to backup files from more than one computer.

➠ **SkyDrive**: Your Microsoft Account comes with gigabytes of free storage in the cloud (on the Internet). Anything stored in SkyDrive is duplicated on additional computers you log into with the same Microsoft Account.

 SkyDrive provides storage but not a backup (duplicate). If you delete a file from SkyDrive, any copies stored on linked computers are also deleted.

In this chapter, you copy files to a flash drive to transport between machines or as an ad hoc backup. You also use the File History function, which automatically copies files as a backup. Consider this scenario: You write a letter to a friend and save it to your documents folder. Later that day, you delete part of the letter and save it again, replacing the original document. The next day, you wish you still had the deleted text. File History comes to your rescue because it saves versions of files; you can recover the latest version or an earlier version of a file. As I wrote this book, I saved it hundreds of times — File History could save every version, allowing me to rollback to an earlier copy, before I made some big goof. (That's purely hypothetical, of course.)

Finally, you explore two tools you may need if you have problems with your computer or you decide to get rid of it. The Refresh function fixes some problems. The Reset function returns your computer to an out-of-the-box condition.

Add an External Hard Drive or Flash Drive

1. Before you attach a flash drive or hard drive to your computer, consider the following options Windows 8 automatically offers for using the newly attached disk:

- **Speed Up My System,** also called ReadyBoost, does what its name implies on computers with 2GB of memory or less. (ReadyBoost is unrelated to copying files.)

See Chapter 12 for system information. Or just try ReadyBoost some other time by inserting a flash drive with more than 2GB free space and then selecting the Speed Up My System option.

- **Configure This Drive for Backup** uses the new drive for the File History function and is best suited to large-capacity drives, at least 500GB. You would select this option to back up all your files.

- **Open Folder to View Files** displays the contents of the disk in File Explorer on the desktop. You would select this option to copy files to or from the drive you're attaching.

- **Take No Action** dismisses the notification.

Notifications appear for the amount of time specified in PC Settings. See Chapter 3 for steps to increase the time that notifications appear on screen. If the notification disappears before you can select it, you can redisplay it by removing and then reinserting the drive or USB cable.

2. Locate an unused USB port on your computer. A *USB port* is a small rectangular slot on the front or back of a desktop computer or along any edge of a laptop or tablet computer. USB ports are often marked with a symbol that looks like a trident, as shown in **Figure 15-1.**

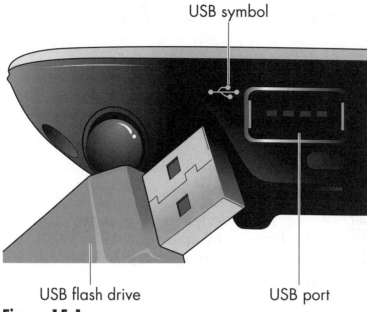

USB symbol

USB flash drive   USB port

Figure 15-1

 If a USB port is hard to reach, you can buy an extension cable from any office supply store. You can also
buy a *hub*, which adds ports to your computer.

3. If you're using a flash drive, insert it into the USB slot —
USB fits one way only. If you're using an external hard
drive, plug it into a power source, if one is required, and
then connect a cable to the USB port. Turn on the external drive, if it has a separate power switch. (Flash drives
and some external hard drives don't have separate power
supplies or switches.)

4. Windows 8 displays a notification to *Tap to choose what
happens with removable drives*. (You can click the mouse
instead of tapping.) If you select the first notification, a
list of choices appears, as shown in **Figure 15-2**. If you
know which action you want to take, you can select that
action. Otherwise, select Take No Action or wait until the
notification disappears on its own.

Figure 15-2

Copy Files to or from a Flash Drive

1. To copy files or folders to a flash drive, insert the flash drive into one of your computer's USB ports.

 Laptops, like cameras, often have a slot for a memory card. Want to turn your memory card into a flash drive? Simply buy a device called a dedicated or single-purpose memory card reader. Strictly speaking a multipurpose card reader would also work, but multicard readers cost more and are often larger than single-card readers. In addition, a dedicated memory card reader lets you skip using a cable to connect a camera to a computer.

2. If Windows 8 displays a notification (refer to **Figure 15-2**) when you insert the flash drive or memory card, select Open Folder to View Files, which will open File Explorer on the desktop. If File Explorer doesn't open automatically, select the Desktop tile on the Start screen, and then select the yellow folder icon in the taskbar.

 The keyboard shortcut to open File Explorer is ⊞+E. You don't need to switch to the desktop before using the shortcut.

3. In File Explorer, navigate on the left to the folder that contains the files you want to copy. See Chapter 14 for information on navigating in File Explorer. Select the folder.

4. On the right side of File Explorer, select the folder or file you want to copy. If you see a check box to the left of each object you want to copy, you can select each check box to copy multiple files at once. (If you don't see check boxes next to files, see Chapter 14 for information on enabling this function for file selection.)

To select every object on the right at once, use the Select All button on the Home tab. You can also select the files you don't want to copy, and then use the Invert Selection button on the Home tab — deselected files become selected and vice versa. You can select files in other ways as well.

The keyboard shortcut to select all files in File Explorer is Ctrl+A.

5. In the ribbon, select the Home tab, and then select the Copy To button, as shown in **Figure 15-3**. Select Choose Location from the menu that appears.

Select the Copy To button

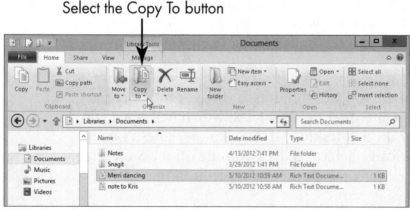

Figure 15-3

You can move files if you want them gone from their original location. To do so, select the Move To button. Follow the remaining steps, but substitute the word *Move* for *Copy*.

6. In the Copy Items window, under the Computer heading, locate the flash drive or memory card. The drive will not be Local Disk (C:), where Windows 8 resides. Select the flash drive or memory card to which you want to copy the files, as shown in **Figure 15-4,** and then select the Copy button. If the files copy quickly, you may not see any indication of progress; otherwise, a progress bar is displayed until copying is complete.

Select a location for the copy

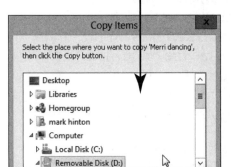

Figure 15-4

 If you select your user name (*mark hinton* in **Figure 15-4**), you may see SkyDrive listed in the expanded list. Files you copy to SkyDrive are automagically copied to the cloud and to linked computers. If you don't see SkyDrive under your user name, see Chapter 14 for steps on installing Windows Essentials (the software that includes SkyDrive).

7. If you copy a file that is already on the destination disk, the Replace or Skip Files window appears, as shown in **Figure 15-5**. (Perhaps you're copying a newer version of a file you copied before.) Note the available options:

- **Replace the File in the Destination Folder:** Selecting this option replaces one file with another. Be certain you don't need the replaced file (as you might if you want to keep different versions of files).

- **Skip This File:** Selecting this option does nothing with this file.

- **Choose the File to Keep in the Destination Folder:** Selecting this option opens another window in which you can select files on the left to replace those on the right and select files on the right to keep. Selecting the same file on the left and right creates a second file with a number added to the name, such as *my file (2)*. This option enables you to have the original and the new file.

Select one of the previous options. If you selected Choose the File to Keep in the Destination Folder, select the files to replace or skip, and then select the Continue button. You may or may not see a progress indicator, depending on how quickly the files are copied.

8. Confirm that the copy worked by navigating on the left to the location you selected as the destination in Step 6. If the files are there, congratulations; you're done. If not, try Steps 4 through 6 again.

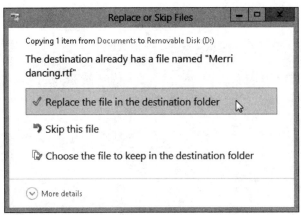

Figure 15-5

9. Remove the flash drive or memory card you inserted in Step 1. You're good to go.

> If you have files or folders that you'd be devastated to lose, follow the steps in this task to create backup copies of those items on a portable storage device. Then keep that device in a safe place.

> To copy files from a flash drive or memory card, follow these same steps but select the flash drive in Step 3 and the library or other destination to which you want to copy or move files in Step 6.

Turn On File History

1. To enable Windows 8 to create backup copies of your files, type **history** on the Start screen. On the search results panel, select Settings and then select File History, as shown in **Figure 15-6**.

> Another way to access File History is to select Configure This Drive for Backup when you attach an external hard drive. In that event, skip to Step 3.

Type your search text here

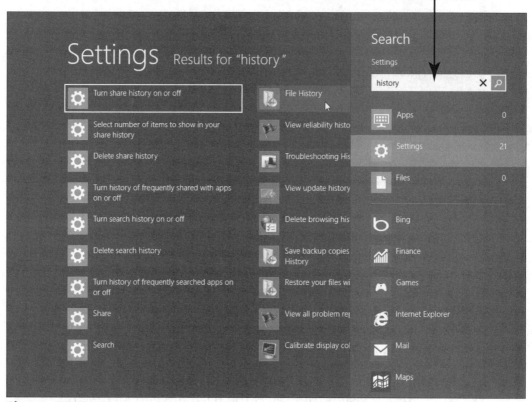

Figure 15-6

 File History stores information on an external drive or a network location. After you turn on File History, it will automatically create copies of your documents and photos on the drive you identify. If you lose, delete, or change your mind about changes to a file, you can restore the backup copy created by File History following the steps in the "Restore Files with File History" section, later in this chapter.

2. The File History window opens on the desktop. (See Chapter 5 for information on using the desktop.) File History is off by default. If an external drive is attached, that drive and its free space appear in the File History window, as shown in **Figure 15-7**. If no drive is displayed, attach one.

Figure 15-7

> Use the Change Drive function if you want to select a different drive for File History. Use an external drive with at least 40GB of free space — the more free space, the better.

3. If the screen indicates that File History is off, select the Turn On button.

4. Select the Advanced Settings function. The screen that appears next (see **Figure 15-8**) provides the following options:

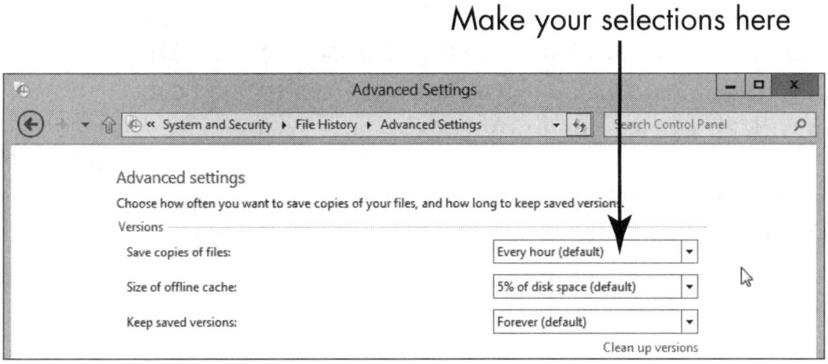

Make your selections here

Figure 15-8

- **Save Copies of Files:** This option controls how frequently File History checks for new or changed files. I recommend that you select Every 10 Minutes to minimize the chances of losing new or changed documents.

- **Size of Offline Cache:** This option applies when you have disconnected the external drive you set up for File History. While that drive is disconnected, an offline cache temporarily stores changes on the internal hard disk. You will probably not need to change this option, especially if you usually leave the external drive attached while you work.

 When you go on vacation, consider disconnecting the external drive and storing it in a fireproof safe or a safe deposit box. The drive is your insurance against theft or destruction.

- **Keep Saved Versions:** By default, File History keeps copies of your files forever. This option allows you to limit how long copies are kept. Leave this set as Forever.

- **Clean Up Versions:** This function opens a window in which you select the time period to use to delete older versions of backups. Times range from older than one month to older than two years. (The Keep Saved Versions option uses the same time increments and performs automatically; this function runs only when you choose it.) The All but the Latest One option, which I do not recommend, does not save any previous versions.

5. If you made changes that you want to keep, select the Save Changes button. Otherwise, select Cancel. You return to the main File History window.

Restore Files with File History

1. On the Start screen, type **restore**. On the search results screen, select Settings on the right. Then select Restore Your Files with File History. File History opens on the desktop, as shown in **Figure 15-9**.

Previous (older) backups

Figure 15-9

> You can also access File History using File Explorer. See Chapter 14 for information on using File Explorer.

2. The most recent backup versions created by File History appear in the window. To see other versions of backups, select the left-pointing arrow at the bottom of the window. To return to the most recent backup, select the right-pointing arrow.

> Don't select the Restore button until you select the specific file(s) you want. Otherwise, all files will be restored at once.

> Generally, you will want to restore the most recent version of a file. However, if you want to restore content that you changed prior to the most recent version, browse to an earlier backup.

3. If you know the location of the file you want to restore, you can open that location with a double-click or double-tap. If you're not sure of the location, select the search box in the upper-right corner and type the document name. Matching results appear as you type. Select the file you want to restore.

 On a touchscreen, the virtual keyboard doesn't appear on the desktop until you select the keyboard icon on the right side of the taskbar.

4. Select the Restore button. If you restored a file you previously deleted, you can close File History. Skip the remaining steps.

5. If the Replace or Skip Files window opens (refer to **Figure 15-5**) in the preceding step, a version of the file exists in the original location. If you're sure you want to restore the previous version of the file, you could choose Replace the File in the Destination Folder. However, to see additional options, select Choose the File to Keep in the Destination Folder. The File Conflicts window appears.

6. In the File Conflicts window, consider the following selections:

- Select files on the left to replace files in the destination with the backup files. (This is the same as selecting Replace on the Replace or Skip Files screen.)

- Select files on the right to cancel restoring those files. (This is the same as selecting Skip on the Replace or Skip Files screen.)

- If you select the same files on both sides of the window, File History will leave the original as is and restore the backup version with the same name plus *(2)*, allowing you to have both versions. (You need this option only if you're uncertain about which version you want.)

If you're restoring multiple files at the same time, you can select different options for each: replace one, skip another, and have File History create a copy for another. That's a lot of choices in one little window.

7. Select Continue, and Windows 8 completes the operation based on your choices in Step 6. The location of the restored files opens in File Explorer.

Refresh a Misbehaving Computer

1. Glitch happens. The computer misbehaves, a program crashes, or the machine becomes unexpectedly slow. If your computer is misbehaving, try refreshing it. On the Start screen, type **refresh**. Select the Settings category and then select the Refresh Your PC tile.

 Before you refresh your PC, see Chapter 12 for information on maintaining Windows 8, especially the Action Center and Reliability Monitor. Updating Windows may resolve some problems.

 The Refresh function should leave your data alone and unchanged. However, consider following Steps 1–3 in the section "Restore Files with File History" to confirm that your external drive contains all your files. Better safe than sorry.

 You can also find this function in the General category of PC Settings screen, under the heading Refresh Your PC without Affecting Your Files. Select the Get Started button.

2. On the Refresh Your PC screen, select the Next button, as shown in **Figure 15-10**.

Figure 15-10

The Refresh function doesn't remove apps installed through the Microsoft Store but does remove any apps you installed any other way. This safety feature is based on the assumption that something you installed from some other source is causing a problem. Be certain that you either don't need a desktop app or you have the materials necessary to reinstall a desktop app, such as Microsoft Office. Windows 8 will create a file on the desktop after the fact identifying the programs it removed.

3. If you see a message to *Insert media*, Windows 8 requires the original installation disc before proceeding. Insert the Windows 8 installation or recover disc in your CD/DVD drive or plug in a USB drive with this information. The Refresh function will proceed when you insert the required media. If you don't have the required media, select Cancel. (Read the remaining steps.)

4. Select the Refresh button. (Or select Cancel, if you're just exploring this feature and don't want to continue with it.)

5. Refresh runs and your computer will restart at least once. When the refresh process is complete, the Lock screen appears. Sign in as usual. Select the Desktop tile. If you see a file named *Removed Apps* on the desktop, double-click or double-tap it to open that file in Internet Explorer. The removed apps are listed. If you're aware that one of these apps created a problem, don't reinstall it.

 Don't be intimidated by the Refresh function — it's easy, quick, and worthwhile if it makes a problem computer run better.

Reset for a Clean Start

1. You may have a reason to return your computer to its pristine out-of-the-box, never-used condition. Perhaps you're giving or selling the computer to someone. Perhaps you like starting over from scratch, especially if something has gone terribly wrong. (Don't worry — that *never* happens. [*rolling eyes*]) On the Start screen, type **reset**. Select the Settings category, and then select the Remove Everything and Reinstall Windows tile.

 Before you reset your computer, make sure you have a complete backup of all your files and programs (other than apps downloaded from the Microsoft Store). Reset will erase all your data. If you turned on File History, follow Steps 1–3 in the section "Restore Files with File History" to confirm that your external drive has all your files. You can use this drive to restore all your files to a new computer (or your current computer, after resetting). Do not reset your computer without a full backup of all your files.

 You can also find this function in the General category of PC Settings screen, under the heading Remove Everything and Reinstall Windows. Select the Get Started button.

2. On the Reset Your PC screen, shown in **Figure 15-11**, select the Next button.

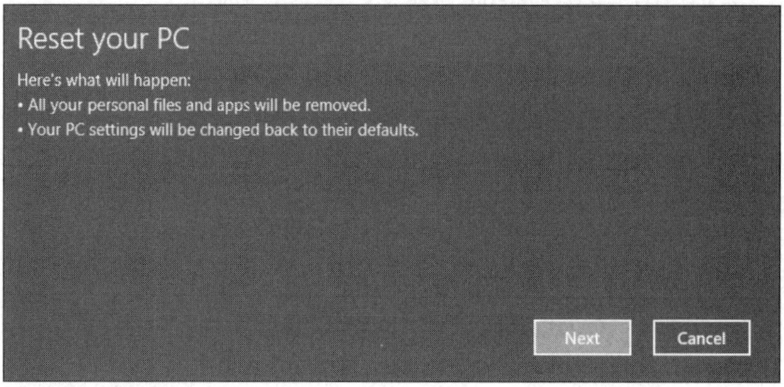

Reset your PC

Here's what will happen:
• All your personal files and apps will be removed.
• Your PC settings will be changed back to their defaults.

Next   Cancel

Figure 15-11

3. If you see a message to *Insert media*, Windows 8 requires the original installation disc before proceeding. Insert the Windows 8 installation or recover disc in your CD/DVD drive or plug in a USB drive with this information. Reset will proceed when you insert the required media. If you don't have the required media, select Cancel here or on the next screen. (Read the remaining steps.)

4. When the computer asks how you want to remove your personal files, select Cancel if you're just exploring this feature. To continue with Reset, select one of the options shown in **Figure 15-12**:

- **Thoroughly, but This Can Take Several Hours:** Select this option if you plan to sell the computer or give it to someone you don't know or trust.

- **Quickly, but Your Files Might Be Recoverable by Someone Else:** Select this option if you're keeping the computer or giving it to someone you know. Your files aren't likely to be recovered by most users other than computer ninjas (like some 15-year-olds or computer science majors).

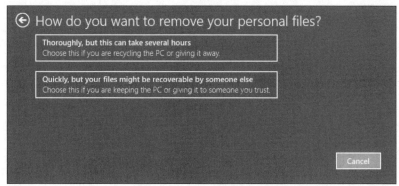

Figure 15-12

5. Reset runs and your computer will restart at least once. When the Reset process is complete, your computer will be in an unused condition. See Chapter 1 to start from scratch. I hope you enjoy the book a second time through. (Programmers call this an *infinite loop*.)

# Index